MW01062415

BREATHE EASY!

A Teen's Guide to Allergies and Asthma

The Science of Health: Youth and Well-Being

Taking Responsibility
A Teen's Guide to Contraception and Pregnancy

Staying Safe
A Teen's Guide to Sexually Transmitted Diseases

What Do I Have to Lose?
A Teen's Guide to Weight Management

Balancing Act
A Teen's Guide to Managing Stress

Surviving the Roller Coaster
A Teen's Guide to Coping with Moods

Clearing the Haze
A Teen's Guide to Smoking-Related Health Issues

Right on Schedule!
A Teen's Guide to Growth and Development

The Best You Can Be
A Teen's Guide to Fitness and Nutrition

The Silent Cry
Teen Suicide and Self-Destructive Behaviors

Breathe Easy!
A Teen's Guide to Allergies and Asthma

Can I Change the Way I Look?
A Teen's Guide to the Health Implications of
Cosmetic Surgery, Makeovers, and Beyond

Taking Care of Your Smile
A Teen's Guide to Dental Care

Dead on Their Feet
Teen Sleep Deprivation and Its Consequences

Dying for Acceptance
A Teen's Guide to Drug- and Alcohol-Related Health Issues

For All to See
A Teen's Guide to Healthy Skin

BREATHE EASY!

A Teen's Guide to
Allergies and Asthma

by Jean Ford

Mason Crest Publishers

Philadelphia

Mason Crest Publishers Inc.
370 Reed Road, Broomall, Pennsylvania 19008
(866) MCP-BOOK (toll free)
www.masoncrest.com

ISBN 1-59084-840-3 (series)

Library of Congress Cataloging-in-Publication Data

Ford, Jean.
  Breathe easy! : a teen's guide to allergies and asthma / by Jean Ford.
    p. cm. — (The science of health)
  ISBN 1-59084-842-X
  1. Allergy—Juvenile literature. 2. Asthma—Juvenile literature. 3. Allergy in children—Juvenile literature. 4. Asthma in children—Juvenile literature. I. Title. II. Series.
  RC585.F675 2004
  616.2'02—dc22
                        2004012779

First edition, 2005
13 12 11 10 09 08 07 06 05   10 9 8 7 6 5 4 3 2

Designed and produced by Harding House Publishing Service, Vestal, NY 13850.
Cover design by Benjamin Stewart.
Printed and bound in India.

This book is meant to educate and should not be used as an alternative to appropriate medical care. Its creators have made every effort to ensure that the information presented is accurate and up to date—but this book is not intended to substitute for the help and services of trained medical professionals.

CONTENTS

INTRODUCTION

by Dr. Sara Forman

You're not a little kid anymore. When you look in the mirror, you probably see a new person, someone who's taller, bigger, with a face that's starting to look more like an adult's than a child's. And the changes you're experiencing on the inside may be even more intense than the ones you see in the mirror. Your emotions are changing, your attitudes are changing, and even the way you think is changing. Your friends are probably more important to you than they used to be, and you no longer expect your parents to make all your decisions for you. You may be asking more questions and posing more challenges to the adults in your life. You might experiment with new identities—new ways of dressing, hairstyles, ways of talking—as you try to determine just who you really are. Your body is maturing sexually, giving you a whole new set of confusing and exciting feelings. Sorting out what is right and wrong for you may seem overwhelming.

Growth and development during adolescence is a multifaceted process involving every aspect of your being. It all happens so fast that it can be confusing and distressing. But this stage of your life is entirely normal. Every adult in your life made it through adolescence—and you will too.

7

Breathe Easy!

But what exactly is adolescence? According to the American Heritage Dictionary, adolescence is "the period of physical and psychological development from the onset of puberty to maturity." What does this really mean?

In essence, adolescence is the time in our lives when the needs of childhood give way to the responsibilities of adulthood. According to psychologist Erik Erikson, these years are a time of separation and individuation. In other words, you are separating from your parents, becoming an individual in your own right. These are the years when you begin to make decisions on your own. You are becoming more self-reliant and less dependent on family members.

When medical professionals look at what's happening physically—what they refer to as the biological model— they define the teen years as a period of hormonal transformation toward sexual maturity, as well as a time of peak growth, second only to the growth during the months of infancy. This physical transformation from childhood to adulthood takes place under the influence of society's norms and social pressures; at the same time your body is changing, the people around you are expecting new things from you. This is what makes adolescence such a unique and challenging time.

Being a teenager in North America today is exciting yet stressful. For those who work with teens, whether by parenting them, educating them, or providing services to them, adolescence can be challenging as well. Youth are struggling with many messages from society and the media about how they should behave and who they should be. "Am I normal?" and "How do I fit in?" are often questions with which teens wrestle. They are facing decisions about their health such as how to take care of

8

their bodies, whether to use drugs and alcohol, or whether to have sex.

This series of books on adolescents' health issues provides teens, their parents, their teachers, and all those who work with them accurate information and the tools to keep them safe and healthy. The topics include information about:

- normal growth
- social pressures
- emotional issues
- specific diseases to which adolescents are prone
- stressors facing youth today
- sexuality

The series is a dynamic set of books, which can be shared by youth and the adults who care for them. By providing this information to educate in these areas, these books will help build a foundation for readers so they can begin to work on improving the health and well-being of youth today.

1

SNIFFING AND SNEEZING:

The Biology of Allergies

What do cats and dogs, peanuts, latex, mold, bee venom, pollen, and shellfish have in common? They're common allergens; in other words, they often cause allergic reactions in people.

Breathe Easy!

With so many—and so ***diverse***—potential triggers, it's no wonder allergies are a major cause of illness and disability in the United States. In fact, they're the sixth leading cause of ***chronic*** disease. Allergies affect as many as one in five adults and children, or about 20 percent of the population. That means for every five people you know, one probably itches, sneezes, or sniffs from something sometime or during certain times of the year. That might include you.

What are allergies? Allergies, in simple terms, are a manifestation of an ***immune system*** in overdrive. Symptoms we usually associate with allergies result from the immune system overreacting to "foreign" substances it encounters (those not normally within the body). These substances are harmless to many people, but the allergic person's body reacts abnormally to that to which he is ***sensitized***. Such substances are called allergens.

Allergens can enter the body through four primary means. Researchers use these four means to classify the allergens:

- **inhalants**: inhaled into the nose and lungs (pollens, mold spores, fungi, dust, dust mites, animal dander, aerosol sprays, smoke, and other pollutants)
- **ingestants**: taken into the body through the mouth (food, food additives, food dyes)
- **contactants**: absorbed through the skin (latex, cosmetic additives, dyes, fabric additives, detergents, some jewelry metals, animal saliva, poison oak or ivy)
- **injectants**: injected directly into the bloodstream or muscle tissue (insect stings, reptile bites, injected or IV drugs).

A peaceful country scene like this is full of some of the most common allergens.

As shown in the list on page 12, many common substances can be allergens. The most common are tree and grass pollens, molds, house dust, dust mites, animal fur and dander, feathers, insect stings, latex, and a variety of foods including soy, dairy, shellfish and nuts (see chapter 2).

What happens when these allergens infiltrate our bodies? Your immune system reacts as a defense mechanism to foreign materials called antigens. Antigens include harmful organisms such as viruses, bacteria, and toxins, as well as generally **benign** substances that produce allergens. An allergen, then, is a type of antigen.

Breathe Easy!

First, an allergen enters your body. Maybe it's late spring and you're cutting the lawn, or maybe it's August and you're at sports camp. By simply being outside you're inhaling microscopic pollens floating in the air. Soon you notice your throat, nose, or eyes becoming itchy. Then you sneeze.

A potential allergen has come in contact with your body. With each breath of fresh air these small particles enter your airways. Your immune system kicks into high gear, thinking your body is under attack, and rushes to identify the foreign invaders. In most people, the immune system quietly protects you by fighting harmful substances. But when you have allergies, it overreacts and "fights" harmless, ordinary things—like pollen or dust—much the same way.

White blood cells called lymphocytes are fundamental components of the immune system. They travel freely among the body's tissues, through blood vessel walls, and between lymph nodes and lymph channels. There are two types of lymphocytes: B-lymphocytes (B-cells) and T-lymphocytes (T-cells). T-cells produce chemicals that play a role in activating other parts of the immune system.

B-cells identify the invaders and ultimately produce ***antibodies*** that are specifically engineered for those allergens. The B-cells are pretty much free to roam everywhere, much like guards on patrol. The B-cells, like security agents, check the I.D. of every cell they encounter. When they discover a stranger in their midst (like pollen) or a foreign substance that seems threatening, they immediately start the process of taking action against it.

First, they perform a microscopic version of "booking" the invader, biochemically fingerprinting the suspect for identification purposes. Once lymphocytes have identified the foreign substance, the cells make their way back to the lymph nodes. There these white blood cells begin producing custom-designed antibodies to protect against that particular threat.

The antibodies, also called immunoglobulin (or Ig), are classified by type. There are five general types of Igs, each identified by a letter suffix: IgA, IgD, IgE, IgG, and IgM. The immunoglobulin responsible for allergic reactions is IgE. Everyone has IgE antibodies, but researchers have found that allergy sufferers have up to ten times as much IgE in their blood as those unaffected by allergies.

In a properly functioning immune system, lymphocytes distinguish between threatening and nonthreatening substances. In a person with allergies, these white blood cells can't make the distinction. For example, harmless, inhaled pollens aren't actually "invading" the body as a virus or bacteria would, but the allergy sufferer's white blood cells respond as if they were, producing and mobilizing large quantities of antibodies—in this case IgE antibodies—to fight the perceived attack. These antibodies, in turn, attach to mast cells, located in the respiratory and gastrointestinal tracts and skin, and basophils, which are found in blood. As many as 500,000 IgE molecules can collect on a single cell. In essence, immune system troops rally to counter a false invasion. They swarm innocent visitors.

You would think that the first time an allergy-prone person comes in contact with an allergen, she would suffer symptoms. That's not usually the case. It takes prior, sensitizing exposure for the mast cells and basophils to become primed with IgE antibodies, and these antibodies—not the allergen—cause the symptoms we suffer. This process of sensitization can take as little as a week or as long as years.

Breathe Easy!

Jena smelled gasoline. Knowing the risk of moving an injured victim, but also realizing the danger gas fumes present, Jena helped lift the victim out of his car and carried him to safety well onto a grassy shoulder. She didn't think twice about kneeling on the leafy ground to support the man's head and neck until EMTs arrived—even though she was in shorts and kneeling in poison ivy. The man survived, but the next day Jena had the worse case of poison ivy she had ever had. Itchy, red bumps were in every nook and cranny imaginable, and she was miserable. "I've walked through poison ivy a thousand times," she lamented to a friend. "I *never* get poison ivy. I thought I was immune."

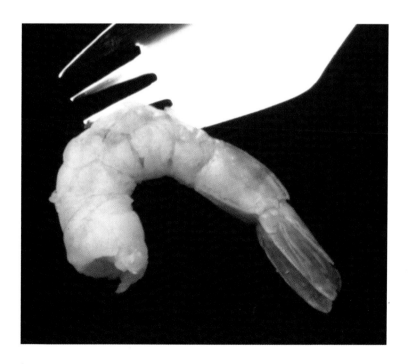

Many people are allergic to shrimp.

The first time the allergy-prone person encounters an allergen, his or her immune system manufactures IgE antibodies to fight that allergen, but doesn't release them. Instead, the antibodies attach to mast cells and basophils in wait for a future exposure.

For example, you eat shrimp for the first time and nothing seems to happen. But, unknown to you, your immune system read the shrimp proteins as threatening your body and produced many shrimp IgE antibodies. These antibodies attached themselves to your cells and stayed there. A few weeks go by. You have shrimp again. This time you have an allergic reaction; maybe you break out in **hives** and your skin itches like mad.

What happened? You ate shrimp a second time, and this time, your immune system was ready. It recognized the threat, and IgE-primed cells used these powerful anti-shrimp antibodies to fight it, releasing chemical **mediators** in the process. Those chemicals caused your reaction. This domino effect within the immune system is called the allergic cascade.

The Culprit

When IgE antibodies and the offending allergens connect during battle, the cells release powerful **inflammatory** chemicals such as histamine, prostaglandins, cytokines, and leukotrienes. Histamine produces many of the familiar allergic symptoms such as itching, sneezing, runny noses, and watery eyes. That's why over-the-counter—OTC—allergy medications include an antihistamine. (*Anti*, which means "against," plus *histamine* equals less histamine, which in turn means fewer symp-

17

toms.) But researchers have determined that some leukotrienes are five to ten *thousand* times more **potent** than histamines in causing airway inflammation and obstruction that may lead to allergy-related breathing issues like asthma (see chapter 4).

Obviously, the discomfort we experience from overly aggressive immune systems varies. The nature and severity of symptoms largely depend on four factors:

1. previous exposure
2. route of exposure (inhaled, ingested, touched, or injected)
3. level of exposure
4. specific type of allergy.

PREVIOUS EXPOSURE

Often the severity of symptoms increases with the number of times you've been exposed to an offending allergen. With each exposure, more and more IgE antibodies are produced. The more antibodies produced, the more chemicals released, and the more released, the greater your symptoms.

ROUTE OF EXPOSURE

Direct contact, such as injecting into the bloodstream, is the purest, quickest, and most dangerous route for allergens to take.

Level of Exposure

This is obvious. Your immune system responds proportionately to threat. If the number of allergens to which you're exposed is high, then the response will be strong. If the number or duration is lessened, so is the reaction. (Brushing up against one poison-ivy leaf would likely result in a less serious case than resting in a bed of it!)

Type of Allergen

Although scientists are not sure why, food allergies (particularly to nuts) are often more severe than environmental allergies like pollen and dust. The difference may lie in the means by which the allergen enters the body—ingested versus inhaled.

Certainly, the severity of reactions involved in stings and bites varies with the species and its venom. A black hornet usually causes a more severe reaction than a yellow jacket. A coral snake bite is generally far more deadly than a rattlesnake's.

Allergy Symptoms

For a few days Craig has had head congestion and a stuffy nose when he wakes up. He can't stop sneezing. When he blows his nose, the mucus is clear, and he otherwise feels fine. *I wonder if I'm getting a cold.*

19

Allergies versus Infections

	Allergies	Infections
Symptoms Can include any or all symptoms listed.	• runny nose • congestion • sneezing • watery eyes • itchy eyes • itchy nose, throat, ears • headache • cough or wheezing • rash or inflammation • swelling • stomach cramps • NO FEVER	• any or all of the allergy symptoms listed • general aches & pains • headache • mild to high fever • chills
Start Time	Symptoms begin on exposure to allergens and can rapidly become severe.	Symptoms generally begin gradually and usually take a few days to hit full force.
Duration	Symptoms remain as long as exposed to the allergen and beyond (until the reaction ends) and can become chronic.	Symptoms clear up within three to ten days regardless of environment.

Sniffing and Sneezing

Because allergy symptoms can mimic colds, viruses, or other conditions, Craig should definitely see a doctor if his symptoms persist for more than a week or so. (See sidebar for help distinguishing between colds and allergies.) The most common allergy symptoms:

- itchy, watery eyes
- itchy, runny nose
- the "allergic salute": pushing up on the end of your nose with your hand or fingers, causing a white crease across the bridge of your nose.
- itchy throat
- sneezing and sniffling
- general itchiness
- hives
- *eczema*
- localized puffiness or swelling
- recurring headaches
- frequent coughing
- wheezing or asthma
- diarrhea and/or stomach cramps

Anaphylactic Shock

Allergies are usually just a nuisance, but occasionally they can pose a life-or-death threat. In some people, allergic responses can lead to anaphylaxis or anaphylactic shock—a sudden and sometimes deadly drop in blood pressure. This can lead to complete closure of air passages, causing death by suffocation, or it can stop the heart.

Breathe Easy!

Because time is essential to treating such reactions, recognizing the early signs of anaphylaxis becomes critical. If you're at risk, educate yourself and those around you! In anaphylactic shock, chemicals released during an allergic reaction overwhelm the body, causing some of the more "normal" allergy symptoms. In fact, the first sign is usually sudden itchiness or swelling. Symptoms progress rapidly: large areas of hives (80 percent of the time), swelling of the throat and/or various parts of the body, **dyspnea**, wheezing, chest tightness, faintness, muddled thinking, feelings of apprehension, and ultimate collapse as blood pressure plummets. All of this can happen in only three or four minutes.

Completely Useless Fact

It's impossible to sneeze with your eyes open.

The best precaution to take is to avoid known allergens. For example, if you know you're allergic to peanuts, don't eat anything with nuts. But it's not that simple. People allergic to nuts must steer clear of anything cooked in peanut oil and avoid restaurants known to use them, even if they claim they don't! Read food labels, note all ingredients, and pay attention to package warnings like, "Warning: this item was packaged in a facility that also processes foods containing nuts or nut oils." But remember, not all products carry these warnings.

People who are allergic to nuts may also be allergic to anything cooked in peanut oil.

Unfortunately, it's not always possible to avoid allergens. Therefore, anyone who has—or even suspects he has—life-threatening allergies should carry an unexpired *EpiPen*® or otherwise equipped *adrenaline kit*. (An EpiPen contains one dosage of epinephrine to be administered in case of an emergency.) Make sure you've discussed how and when to use your kit with your physician *before* needing to use it. Fumbling with the "how to's" during a crisis wastes valuable time. One pre-measured dose of adrenaline increases blood pressure, restor-

23

Five Anaphylactic Myths

Myth #1: Anaphylaxis becomes increasingly more severe with each episode.

Fact: *There is no predictable pattern with anaphylaxis. Episodes can be the same, more severe, or even less severe depending on exposure and whether your body has become more or less allergic.*

Myth #5: Anaphylaxis is easy to prevent just by avoiding known allergens.

Fact: *Avoiding allergens is certainly wise, but most cases of anaphylaxis occur due to accidental exposure. Therefore, it is never safe to be without your medication if you're at risk, even if taking other precautions.*

Myth #3: Taking an antihistamine like Benadryl® before eating problem foods can prevent anaphylaxis.

Fact: *Although it's possible to lessen mild allergic reactions with medicine, preventing anaphylaxis isn't possible. In fact, antihistamines can conceal early phases of a reaction (like hives) that normally serve as your warning signs. The absence of these "red flags" increases the risk of a dangerous outcome.*

Myth #4: Anaphylaxis takes at least twenty minutes to begin, so there is always time to get treatment.

Fact: *Reactions can be immediate, even within seconds of ingesting an allergen. It's also important to remember that treatment can be less effective if delayed.*

Myth #2: All cases of anaphylaxis are life threatening.

Fact: *Some cases are quite mild and go away without treatment. But because severity is impossible to predict, every episode must be taken seriously.*

ing it to normal, and reduces swelling, particularly in the airways. Don't leave home without it!

Although the immediate emergency situation can be **alleviated** with an injection of adrenaline, you should still seek medical attention as soon as possible.

Another note about adrenaline: it doesn't last forever. It can expire with time, and it definitely deteriorates in sunlight. If adrenaline looks discolored or cloudy, it's lost potency. Replace it immediately; don't wait. Always check the expiration date on any medication, but especially EpiPens® or their equivalent. Outdated adrenaline loses potency and can become ineffective.

In addition to carrying an adrenaline kit, you should let others know about your allergy, and you should con-

> ## Hyping History
>
> • The term "allergy" was first used in 1906 and referred to any unusual reaction— helpful or harmful—within the immune system.
> • In 1966, Kimishige and Teruko Ishizaka at the Children's Asthma Research Institute of Denver discovered the IgE antibody and its effects.

sider wearing a medical I.D. tag or bracelet. These are like "dog tags" worn by the military. If you should lose consciousness during a severe allergic reaction, the tag can speak for you, providing necessary medical alerts to assure the best possible treatment. That can save your life.

Allergic Disease and Its Causes

An overreactive immune system is more formally known as allergic disease. Even though this illness has been identified for more than a hundred years, scientists and doctors still don't know why the immune system overreacts as it does.

Researchers do know that there's a definite, genetic (or inherited) component to allergic disease. If one parent has allergies, chances are one in three (33 percent) that their children will develop an allergy. If both parents have allergies, the chances increase to seven in ten (70 percent). But please note, although the *tendency* toward allergies is genetic, specific allergies are not. Even though you may be born with a genetic **propensity** toward having allergies, you're not automatically allergic to any specific allergen. You must be exposed to the allergen to become allergic to it.

What are the most common allergic diseases? According to the Asthma and Allergy Foundation of America (AAFA), there are thirteen.

Allergic Rhinitis (Hay Fever)

This is characterized by nasal stuffiness, sneezing, nasal itching, clear nasal discharge, and itching of the roof of the mouth and/or ears.

Allergic Asthma

The defining symptom for allergic asthma is airway obstruction that is at least partially reversible with medication and is always associated with allergy. Symptoms include coughing, wheezing, shortness of breath or rapid breathing, chest tightness, occasional fatigue, and slight chest pain.

Allergic Conjunctivitis

Eye inflammation is the most common form of allergic eye disease. Symptoms can include itchy and watery eyes and lid distress. Allergic conjunctivitis is also commonly associated with the presence of other allergic diseases such as *atopic* dermatitis, allergic rhinitis, and asthma.

Breathe Easy!

Urticaria is a skin reaction that causes the development of hives surrounded by an area of red inflammation. Acute urticaria is often caused by an allergy to foods or medication.

> ## Allergy Quiz
>
> Which of the following puts you at risk for developing allergies?
>
> Your girlfriend has allergies.
> You volunteer at a local hospital.
> You have a cat.
> You live in a rural area.
> Your biological brother is allergic to peanuts, dust, and bee stings.
>
> *Answer:*
> *Allergies are not contagious, so your girlfriend and the hospital are out. Since you can't develop allergies to specific allergens without a genetic predisposition to do so, the cat and area where you live are out. But since your brother has allergies, and he came from the same genetic pool you did, chances are you inherited similar propensities. That puts you at increased risk for developing some form of allergic disease.*

28

Atopic Dermatitis (Eczema)

This chronic or recurrent inflammatory skin disease is characterized by *lesions*, scaling, and flaking; it is sometimes called eczema. In children, it may be aggravated by an allergy, irritant, or even emotional stress.

Contact Dermatitis

Contact dermatitis is one of the most common skin diseases in adults. It results from the direct contact by the skin with an outside substance such as poison ivy. There are currently about 3,000 known contact allergens.

Sinusitis

This inflammation of the sinuses frequently mimics the common cold, but the symptoms of sinusitis persist for a longer period of time than a typical cold. Fever may develop or persist. Symptoms of sinusitis include frontal head discomfort, facial pain that often worsens when patients are bending or straining, and yellow or green nasal discharge.

Otitis Media (Middle Ear Infection)

Inflammation can occur in both the middle ear and the eardrum. A middle-ear infection is the most common childhood disease requiring physician care. As many as half of the children over three years of age with chronic otitis media also have confirmed allergic rhinitis.

FOOD ALLERGY

This is most prevalent in very young children, and it is frequently outgrown. Food allergies are characterized by a broad range of allergic reactions. Symptoms may include itching or swelling of lips or tongue; hives; tightness of the throat with hoarseness; nausea and vomiting; diarrhea; occasionally, chest tightness and wheezing; itching of the eyes; decreased blood pressure; or loss of consciousness and anaphylaxis.

LATEX ALLERGY

An allergic response to the proteins in natural latex rubber is characterized by a range of allergic reactions. Symptoms include hand dermatitis, eczema, and urticaria; sneezing and other respiratory distress; and lower respiratory problems, including coughing, wheezing, and shortness of breath. Persons at risk include healthcare workers, patients having multiple surgeries, and rubber-industry workers.

ANAPHYLAXIS

Because anaphylaxis is characterized by life-threatening symptoms, it is a medical emergency and the most severe form of allergic reaction. Symptoms include a sense of impending doom; generalized warmth or flush; tingling of palms, soles of feet, or lips; lightheadedness; bloating; and chest tightness. These can progress into **seizures**, **cardiac arrhythmia**, **shock**, and respiratory distress. Possible causes can be medications, vaccines, food, latex, and insect stings and bites.

INSECT STING ALLERGY

Characterized by a variety of allergic reactions, stings are usually unexpected and can happen to anyone. Symptoms include pain, itching, and swelling at the sting site or over a larger area. Anaphylaxis can occur. Insects that sting include bees, hornets, wasps, yellow jackets, and fire and harvest ants.

DRUG ALLERGY

Drugs can cause a variety of allergic responses affecting any tissue or organ. Drug allergies can cause anaphylaxis; even those patients who do not have life-threatening symptoms initially may progress to a life-threatening reaction.

Obviously allergies and allergens are widespread and diverse. In the next two chapters we take a closer look the most common allergens.

2

SURROUNDED!

Environmental Allergens

Scott was excited to make the football team, but he knew August was going to be brutal. Two-hour practices, five days a week, rain or shine! That was a lot of drills.

But long hours on a hot football field turned out to be the least of Scott's problems. His allergies, too, had a field day. *How can I keep playing,* he silently lamented. *I can't concentrate when this itching is driving me crazy.*

Megan loved her new job. Waiting tables at the Rustic was the best! Great food, an oft-used fireplace, down-to-earth customers who tipped well, and walls dotted with every imaginable mining antique woven together to create an undeniably desirable atmosphere in which to work. But there was a hitch. Every time Megan entered the restaurant, her throat and nose began to itch. She'd even sneezed more than once on an order. *What am I going to do,* she wondered. *I can't keep this up or I'll be fired.*

Allergens are everywhere. They're all around us. As we discussed in the last chapter, they enter the body in four distinct ways: being inhaled, ingested, injected, or coming in contact with your skin. We'll cover ingested, injected, and contact allergens in the next chapter; for now let's examine inhaled allergens. These allergens are found in the everyday environments: our homes, yards, schools, churches, stores, businesses, and parks.

What are common environmental allergens? Pollens, mold spores, dust, dust mites, and animal dander. Let's tackle pollens first.

Pollens

Pollens are microscopic particles produced by plants at various times of the year, particularly in the spring and

Flower pollen can trigger an allergic reaction in human beings.

fall months. These pollens are discharged by many kinds of plants—including weeds, trees and grasses—for the purpose of ***propagation***. Pollens travel from plant to plant on the slightest breeze. Being airborne, they become part of the air we breathe and cause many allergies of the nose, eyes, and lungs.

When we inhale, pollens settle into the lining of our nose, throat, and lungs. As we learned in the last chapter, if you're allergic, the first time you encountered a specific pollen, your white blood cells detected its presence, identified it, and then produced antibodies designed to neutralize it that then attached to mast cells and basophils, and waited. The next time you were exposed to the same pollen, these antibody-laden cells were ready. They rushed to affected tissues—your nose and throat—and battled the pollen with the antibodies, releasing histamine in the process. Histamine causes the lining of the nose, sinuses, eyelids, eyes, and even our throat or air passageways to swell and become irritated. That's why we itch and sneeze, and, for some, feel tight in our chests.

Such allergy attacks can last as little as fifteen to twenty minutes or for as long as a few days. Most attacks continue as long as the untreated allergy sufferer remains exposed to offending allergen(s). For most patients, pollen allergies are merely annoying, but for a few, they become debilitating, interfering with daily life and even causing potentially life-threatening symptoms like severe swelling in the throat or asthma.

Completely Useless Fact

Because symptoms worsen for many allergy sufferers during spring and early fall—traditional times of hay harvesting—pollen allergies earned the informal name "hay fever."

Which trees, grasses, or weeds are the most common pollen-producing culprits? According to the American Academy of Allergy, Asthma, and Immunology, there are many. Check out the following table and try to identify plants that grow in your area.

Because pollen particles can travel significant distances on the wind, it is important for you not only to understand your immediate, local environment but also the conditions in the region where you live. "Allergy capitals" are identified and ranked each year by the Asthma and

ALLERGEN SOURCE	PLANT SPECIES
Weeds	Burning Bush Carlessweeds English Plantain Lamb's Quarters Ragweed Redroot Pigweed Russian Thistle (a.k.a. tumbleweed) Sagebrush
Grasses	Bahai Grass Bermuda Grass Johnson Grasses Kentucky Bluegrass Orchard Grass Redtop Grass Sweet Vernal Grass Timothy Grass
Trees	Alder Ash Box Elder Elm Hickory Mountain Cedar Mulberry Oak Pecan Sycamore Walnut

Breathe Easy!

Allergy Foundation of America. These rankings indicate the fifty worst cities in the U.S. for seasonal allergies during peak times of the year: spring and fall. We've listed the ten worst cities for these seasons in 2003 (please see charts on pages 39 and 40). Environmental and medical factors are considered in assigning rank:

- average recorded spring and fall pollen counts over the previous year
- length of the peak season for the most offensive pollens
- number of antihistamine prescriptions issued per capita over the year
- number of board-certified ***allergists*** per capita for that year.

The most intense times for weed, grass, and tree pollens vary across the country according to climate, growing seasons, and allergen type. Springtime allergies are often due to tree pollens. Allergies that occur in early summer are usually grass triggered. For fall allergies, weeds such as ***ragweed*** are likely culprits. You can check out pollen forecasts online on many weather Web sites. Just click on the city nearest you.

Pollen counts also vary with the time of day and weather conditions. They're usually lowest after a rain and in the late afternoon and evening. The highest pollen counts occur in hot, dry, windy weather and between 4:00 and 10:00 A.M.

If you find yourself sniffing and sneezing in spring or fall, you're not alone. Pollen allergies are one of the most prevalent chronic diseases in America, affecting about 10 percent of American residents. For every ten people you know, there is probably at least one person who has seasonal pollen allergies.

38

Surrounded!

Top Ten Worst Spring Allergy Cities (U.S.) for 2003

SPRING 2003 Ranking	Designated Market Area (DMA)	FINAL SPRING SCORE	Pollen Level Score	Pre-scrip-tion Score	Aller-gist Score
1	Louisville, KY	100	94.24	86.83	67.49
2	Austin, TX	97.21	99.89	73.56	91.96
3	St. Louis, MO	96.84	100	63.96	47.65
4	Atlanta, GA	96.68	99.89	56.46	33.66
5	Charlotte, NC	96.55	97.56	73.93	76.66
6	Hartford, New Haven, CT	96.43	92.02	84.3	88.31
7	Nashville, TN	96.11	84.26	95.36	79.55
8	Raleigh-Durham-Fayetteville, NC	94.67	80.38	100	96.75
9	Harrisburg-Lancaster-Lebanon-York, PA	94.14	83.37	88.89	62.25
10	Grand Rapids-Kala-mazoo-Battle Creek, MI	89.04	79.38	81.96	59.99

Top Ten Worst Fall Allergy Cities (U.S.) for 2003

FALL 2003 Ranking	Designated Market Area (DMA)	FINAL FALL SCORE	Pollen Level Score	Prescription Score	Allergist Score
1	Harrisburg-Lancaster-Lebanon-York, PA	100	92.76	88.89	62.25
2	Raleigh-Durham-Fayetteville, NC	99.33	87.93	100	96.75
3	Louisville, KY	98.87	92.87	86.83	67.49
4	Austin, TX	97.05	100	73.56	91.96
5	Grand Rapids-Kalamazoo-Battle Creek, MI	94.37	87.93	81.96	59.99
6	Memphis, TN	93.94	99.2	66.32	86.25
7	Oklahoma City, OK	93.77	96.32	58.71	38.58
8	Dallas-Ft.Worth, TX	93.46	95.52	68.10	69.86
9	Kansas City, MO	93.13	95.52	68.10	69.86
10	St. Louis, MO	92.65	93.91	63.96	47.65

What can pollen sufferers do? Although the almost forty million of us who suffer seasonal allergies can't move to another planet, we can decrease our pollen exposure. Try taking the following steps, especially during high pollen-count days, to minimize the pollens you encounter:

1. Stay indoors if you can. Avoid outdoor activities during the morning hours when pollen counts are highest, especially on dry, windy days. If you must be active outside, try wearing a pollen or dust mask. It might look dorky, but your immune system will spare you.
2. Close all windows and doors, and run a **HEPA air filter** or room purifier.
3. Spend as much time as possible in air-conditioned places. Museums, libraries, theaters, and malls are great alternatives if you don't have air conditioning at home.
4. When driving, close car windows tightly and turn on the air conditioner.
5. If you have central air in your home, or window air conditioning units, make sure to clean and replace filters regularly.
6. Remove clothes and shoes when you come in from outdoors so you don't track pollen around the house, onto furniture, or into your bedroom.
7. Shower or bathe before going to bed each night to wash off any pollen that might have collected on your hair or skin. Washing pollens away avoids transferring them to hands, pillows, and sheets.
8. Use a clothes dryer during allergy seasons instead of hanging clothes outside to dry, espe-

41

cially sheets and pillowcases. Items on a clothesline act like giant filters, trapping pollens in the breeze. The fabric gets saturated with these windborne particles, and then we put our heads on it. No wonder we sneeze!

Even taking the best precautions cannot eliminate pollen exposure all together. Determining what we're allergic to and then treating those allergies accordingly is the next step. Allergy testing is readily available through your doctor and can be conducted in various ways. (Please see chapter 6: Tools and Treatments.) Relief from allergy symptoms can be found in treatments as basic as OTC antihistamines or as complicated as regimens of prescription meds and shots. (Again, see chapter 6.)

Educate yourself on whatever steps you and your doctor agree on. Know the side effects of any drug you take. Check with your pharmacist for any possible drug interactions. Then follow the prescribed course as directed. Some people—a very few—do not respond to treatment. Most find relief. You can, too!

Dust and Dust Mites

Here we must clarify. If you're dust sensitive, chances are you're not allergic to "dust" at all. More likely, it's what's *in* dust that triggers your symptoms. Household dust, as most think of it, is comprised of other allergens like mold spores, fibers, pollen, animal dander, and dead dust mites and their waste. *Those* are the particles you see floating in shafts of sunlight, not just dust at all. For many, the worst of these allergens are dust mites.

The average human will have shed ten pounds of skin by the time he is twenty, a virtual dust mite buffet.

What are dust mites? Think B-movie horror flick: prehistoric **arachnids** swarming the living areas of people, feasting on dead flesh. Is it fiction? Not at all! Invisibly lurking in our carpets, sofas, drapes, and beds—especially in our sheets, pillows, blankets, and stuffed animals—are creatures so small that you need a microscope to see them. Do they eat our flesh? You bet. These tiny creatures are called dust mites.

Dust mites are the tiniest bugs of the arachnid family, —measuring about one hundredth of an inch in length. (That's much smaller than the period at the end of this sentence.) They thrive in warm, humid environments and feast on the microscopic flakes of skin that all humans shed. Consequently, most dust mites in your home live in your mattress and pillow. Frankly, most beds ***teem*** with them. Yuk.

Beyond the obvious gross factor, what's the big deal? We don't even see dust mites, so can't we coexist? For most people, the answer is no. Dust mite droppings are a major cause of allergies and asthma across the continent. These bugs' bathroom habits make us sick—literally! Their waste is a significant allergen responsible for many allergy attacks. And it's almost everywhere.

Because mites thrive in humid conditions, if you happen to live in drier and cooler climates, like that of Saskatchewan or Colorado, you're in luck. Dust mites are virtually nonexistent there, or at least not as bad as in places where humidity is high like Vancouver, Oregon, New Jersey, or Alabama. Humid seasons like spring and early summer also compound the problem. So do rainy spells, when dust mite populations explode.

Short of moving, what can the allergic person do? Lots! Just like with pollens, the key is minimizing exposure. Take steps to reduce humidity levels in your home. Mites grow best at 70 to 80 percent ***relative humidity***, but cannot survive in less than 50 percent, so maintaining an indoor humidity below that will greatly reduce dust mite numbers. Invest in a good ***dehumidifier*** and use it, particularly in your bedroom. Running an air conditioner throughout warm, humid seasons will also decrease mite counts.

Next, as dust-mite central, attack your bedroom. Put airtight plastic or polyurethane covers on all mattresses and box springs. (If possible, keep only one bed in the room.) Zipper-covers that encase the entire mattress, top and bottom, rather than those that merely stretch over the top are best. Encase synthetic pillow(s) likewise. Pillowcases and sheets go on over these covers.

Remove feather pillows and any nonwashable comforters from the room. Launder all bedding—sheets, mattress pads, pillowcases, blankets, and bedspreads—weekly. Make sure you wash it in very hot water, at least 130 degrees Fahrenheit (54 degrees Celsius). Lesser temperatures don't kill dust mites. If your hot water heater is set lower to avoid accidental scalding (commonly 120 degrees Fahrenheit, or 49 degrees Celsius), take advantage of commercial laundries that use high wash temperatures.

Most people don't like this next tip: remove the carpeting! It's just one giant dust trap. Carpeting makes dust mite control impossible, therefore health care experts recommend replacing it with hardwood floors, tile, or linoleum; polished floors are best. Make sure to damp mop or wipe floor surfaces frequently.

If you must have carpeting, try not to install it over concrete. The warm space between rugs and concrete is a good place for mites to live. Vacuum all rugs regularly, at least weekly, and use a vacuum cleaner with a high-efficiency particulate absorption (HEPA) or *electrostatic filter*.

If you just can't rip out your bedroom carpeting, there are means of treatment available, but be warned: they're far less effective at controlling dust mites than removing the carpet itself. You can spray your rug with a solution of 3 percent *tannic acid* every two months. If your doctor recommends using this solution, he or she can tell you where to obtain it and how to apply it. There are also dry, powdered "sprinkle and vac" *miticides* that you can use to treat your room more frequently.

Replace all upholstered furniture with pieces made of wood, plastic, vinyl, or leather, and wipe them often with a damp cloth. Many allergists recommend shades or drapes rather than mini-blinds, since the latter are dust magnets. Keep all clothing in sealed containers or zippered, plastic bags in a closet with the door shut as much as possible. Place all plush toys and stuffed animals on the shelf in that closed closet. Remove "dust collectors" like books and trophies to other rooms.

Dust and vacuum often! Wipe all surfaces—including tops of doors, windows, baseboards, and picture frames—with a damp cloth to avoid stirring up the dust and launching it into the air. Vacuuming and dusting can release large numbers of allergens into the air, so you'll want to take precautions against inhaling them. Wear a well-fitted dust mask when housecleaning.

Although these steps may seem extreme or even difficult at first, experience and ultimately "habit" will make them easier. Easier breathing, fewer meds, and freedom from allergy or asthma attacks are the immeasurable benefits from the additional effort.

Mold and Mold Spores

His first trip to the Jersey shore! Kyle couldn't wait. He and his friends had rented his aunt's new, two-story condo right on the beach. The weather forecast was good, and the surf was supposed to be high—perfect for boarding. *Ah, a week in paradise*, or at least that's what Kyle thought. Within moments of arriving, Kyle was miserable.

First he noticed the sniffles as he unpacked. Then a dry cough set in, and his chest grew tight. Fatigue overwhelmed him as his oxygen levels dipped, and all he felt up to doing was lying on the couch. At first he thought he was getting sick, but the symptoms came on so suddenly,

46

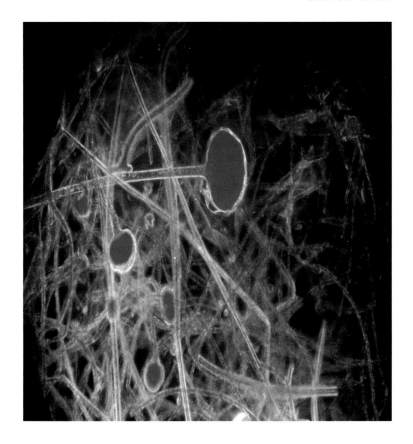

Microscopic mold cells.

and he didn't have a fever. Initially puzzled, the lightbulb eventually lit. *Molds! That must be it.* He knew he was allergic to molds, but he never expected to encounter them here.

"The **spore count** must be high," Kyle commented to his friends as he reached for his allergy meds and inhalers. "I thought this place smelled musty."

Have you ever seen green fuzzies growing on the cheese in your fridge, or on old rolls or a loaf of bread? Maybe

47

Molds come in many shapes and colors.

you've even grown some in a Petri dish for a biology lab. In either case, that fuzzy stuff is mold.

Molds are microscopic fungal organisms. (Yes, they're living *fungi*.) They mature as their fine, thread-like structures spread on and into *organic* materials like food, paper, cardboard, leather, and natural fabrics. When clusters of these filaments get large enough, they become visible as fuzzy growths. *Mildew* on tile grout is a great example of visible mold.

Molds actually feed on organic matter, breaking it down with secreted enzymes. These enzymes convert the matter into nutrients the molds need to survive. This "breaking down" makes molds damaging. Have you ever left a beach towel or damp gym clothes in a duffle bag for more than a day or two? What about those books stored in a cardboard box in the basement? Chances are they've all developed musty odors and maybe even greenish-brown stains here or there. That's the beginning of mold damage.

Unlike plants that need energy from the sun to produce food, molds obtain their energy by digesting other organic matter. They live off of other living things. To do so requires moisture, so molds like damp locations.

You can easily spot patches of mold in tree bark, rotting logs, mulch piles, under grass clippings, inside hay bales, or on the underside of fallen leaves and other decaying vegetation. Rotting food and standing trash are also common sites. Unlike plant pollens, outdoor molds don't have clearly defined seasons, but they do tend to peak during warm, humid times of the year. Conversely, if snow is on the ground, outside mold sources cease.

Indoors, molds love dark, dank basements and poorly ventilated bathrooms with little natural light. They tend to *proliferate* where moisture collects. Shower curtains, tile grout, window moldings, walls, refrigerators, trash cans, and cellars are favorite spots.

As with pollens and dust mite waste, mold spores, another common allergen, are routinely inhaled. Molds reproduce by forming spores that, like pollens, travel through the air, settle onto organic matter, and begin growing new clusters. These airborne spores are the "molds" we inhale. They, too, can travel over large distances and usually outnumber pollen particles.

As with all allergens, decreasing exposure is critical for those allergic to mold spores. Because mold needs moisture to thrive, dehumidify! That's key. Control indoor humidity levels with an air conditioner or a dehumidifier.

Breathe Easy!

Thirty-five to 40 percent relative humidity is ideal, but never go over 50 percent. You can usually purchase a humidity gauge wherever barometers and thermometers are sold.

Clean areas where molds are likely to flourish frequently. Thoroughly scrub shower curtains, tile, toilet tanks, damp walls and ceilings, window sills, refrigerators, and trash cans with a two-to-one mixture of water to chlorine bleach, or use comparable spray cleaners. Some cleaners have mold-killing additives or mold inhibitors. Look for those.

Don't carpet bathrooms, basements, or other rooms prone to dampness. Linoleum is a far better choice for the allergy sufferer. Decorate walls with mold-resistant paint instead of wallpaper. Turn on the exhaust fan or open a window while showering or bathing to allow extra steam and humidity to escape. Squeegee shower walls when done.

These steps can certainly minimize exposure to inside molds, but what about outside ones? Can you ever enjoy the great outdoors again? Certainly! Just use your head.

When planning outdoor activities, remember "dry regions, dry seasons." For example, hiking the Rockies in mid-summer is a far better choice than canoeing the Everglades in spring. Avoid camping where mold growth is likely to be high. Yes, dense forests, lake regions, and swamps are prime locations for molds, but most campgrounds and parks have open, grassy areas free of rotting logs, leaves, or other vegetation. Stick to those sites.

With a little effort, the mold-allergy sufferer can move about his or her world as if allergy free. Like preventatives for dust allergies, these measures may seem burdensome at first, but before you know it, the tasks become routine. Most allergic people find enormous relief just taking these actions, but as with all allergies, medical intervention might be necessary for some. (Please see Chapter Six: Tools and Treatments for further information.)

PET DANDER

Pet *dander* is our last "environmental" allergen. Environmental? Animals? Why? Because the allergen to which we respond is not the animal itself, rather it's its dander—bits of dead skin flakes that all animals shed. This dander, like dust mite waste, gets into common house dust, carpeting, upholstered furniture, and the air we breathe; hence the environmental characteristic.

Animal-born allergens can also be found in an animal's saliva and urine. Contrary to popular belief, however, animal hair or fur is not a significant allergen. The confusion might be traced to the fact that hair and fur often act as collection sites for pollen, dust, and mold spores. When we come in contact with the fur, we encounter these other allergens.

It was the holidays. Josh couldn't wait to have his brother Jerry and sister-in-law Marie over. After all, that's why he got this place. *But what about Jasper*, he worried. *Marie's allergic to dogs. . . . I know what I can do . . . I'll just board him for the weekend*, Josh rationalized. *That should help. It's not too late to get him in.*

We're exposed to animal allergens in two ways: through direct contact with the animal—petting, handling, or even getting or giving "kisses"—and by merely being in rooms where microscopic dander is present. As logical

51

> ## Pet Points
>
> - The number of pets in the United States is estimated at 100,000,000.
> - More than 70 percent of U.S. households have a dog or cat.
> - Approximately six million Americans are allergic to cats, and one-third of them still have cats in their homes.
> - The most common household pets are dogs, cats, birds, hamsters, rabbits, mice, gerbils, rats, and guinea pigs.
> - The best pets for allergic individuals are those without hair or fur and those that don't shed dander. Tropical fish are ideal.

and well intentioned as Josh was, Marie was in trouble. Removing pets as a short-term solution usually doesn't help the pet-allergic because it takes four weeks or more (even months) for dander to lose potency. In addition, dander gets into upholstered furniture and is impossible to remove.

When a family member develops allergies to a beloved animal, the situation can be traumatizing. It's certainly emotionally charged. Obviously the most effective treatment is removing the pet from the home, but many families just can't do that, even for the health and well-being of one of their members.

If you or a family member has animal allergies and your family is unwilling to remove the pet, the animal should at least be kept out of the allergic person's bedroom and restricted to as few rooms in the home as possible. If at all doable, the best compromise is to move the pet outdoors.

Here are a few other strategies for minimizing exposure to animal allergens when the animal still lives with you.

- Allergic individuals should pet, scratch, rub, handle, hug, or kiss their pets as little as possible.
- Bathe your pets regularly, using anti-allergen shampoos.
- Wear a dust mask when cleaning cages, bedding, or litter boxes.
- Change your pet's bedding and litter frequently.
- Place litter boxes and cages away from areas connected to the home's air supply.
- Run air filters, air purifiers, and/or air conditioning units to remove dander-saturated dust particles from the air.

By employing these simple measures, you and your pets may be able to coexist and live happily ever after.

3

SURPRISED!

Additional Allergens

Lou took Rosie to the new Chinese restaurant on their first date. He heard the food was excellent and at prices a struggling student could afford. It was the perfect choice for a perfect evening—until his throat began to swell. The last thing Lou remembered before blacking out was how much he was enjoying himself.

Environmental allergies. Food allergies. Allergies to medicines. Almost anything can become an allergen under the right circumstances with the right person, even sunlight or a fetus in utero. (Yes, a few, rare moms— very few—actually develop allergies to their children during pregnancy!) In this chapter, we deal with the most common, nonenvironmental allergens: specific foods, medicines, occupational hazards, and latex. Let's start with the most common and potentially the most severe: food.

In our opening case, Lou ingested food cooked in oils made from his particular allergen: peanuts. No, he didn't intentionally order or eat anything with "nuts"; he knew better than that. But the General Tso's Chicken he thought was safe was prepared, unbeknownst to him, in peanut oil. How could he have known?

Food allergies are often the most dangerous for two reasons: first, the means by which the allergen enters the body (ingestion), and second, the hidden quality of ingredients, especially those in foods prepared by others. Consequently, many food-related allergy attacks are accidental. Allergic individuals simply don't know their allergens are in the tasty treats they're eating.

It may be helpful to distinguish between genuine food allergies and food intolerance at this point. Many people have an unpleasant reaction to something they ate and immediately assume "food allergy!" Actually, only about five to eight percent of children and even fewer adults— just 2.5 percent—have clinically proven, allergic responses to foods. Bona fide food allergies are relatively rare, especially when compared to environmental aller-

Menacing Munchies?

- Some Orange Julius® beverages contain Julius Smoothy Booster, which contains almond bitters.
- Wendy's® and many other fast-food restaurants have added prepared salads to their menus. Healthy, right? Not for individuals with nut allergies. The Mandarin Chicken Salad™ contains almonds, and the Spring Mix™ contains pecans.
- Ice cream shops routinely use the same utensils to serve nut-enhanced treats as they do more "safe" offerings.
- Warner-Lambert Company manufactures Trident Advantage and Trident for Kids gums. Both contain Recaldent to strengthen teeth. It contains milk.
- Mini Ritz Bite-Size Crackers list milk on the label. Regular Ritz Crackers do not.

gies like hay fever. However, food allergies' prevalence has increased by 55 percent in the last five years.

So what's the difference between allergy and intolerance? As with other allergies, food allergy is an abnormal response of the immune system to an allergen, in this case a specific food. Food intolerance is a physical reaction to a food or food additive that may not involve the immune system at all.

For example, a person experiences uncomfortable abdominal symptoms after drinking milk. The cramping, gas, and indigestion that the person feels is most likely caused by *lactose* intolerance, not an allergy. They sim-

> ## WATCH OUT!
>
> That "secret ingredient" could kill you. Here are a few examples:
>
> - hot chocolate made with peanut butter
> - specialty coffees containing tree nuts, eggs, or milk
> - tuna packaged in soy protein or casein (a milk derivative)
> - nutless cereals with almond meal
> - "harmless" varieties of ice cream processed by equipment shared with nut- or berry-containing varieties
> - deli meats cut on slicers that also cut cheese slices
> - pastas containing egg
> - skin-care products that use crushed shells from nuts or shellfish as an exfoliating agent

ply lack the enzymes to break down milk sugars for proper digestion, and that makes digestion more difficult causing discomfort. Here the immune system is not involved at all. An allergy is not responsible for the symptoms.

Why is this distinction important? A person with allergies to food must avoid all sources of the allergen, even minute amounts. He or she also shouldn't handle the allergen or otherwise touch it (like peeling shrimp or shelling nuts).

On the other hand, the person with food intolerance is often able to ingest modified portions or types of the offending food, especially if he or she uses OTC preparations designed to replace and/or function like the missing enzymes. Handling the food presents no problem.

> **Completely Useless Fact**
>
> It takes a normal, healthy stomach an hour to break down cow milk.

It is extremely important for people who have true food allergies to identify their ingested allergens. Since allergic reactions to food can cause devastating illness and, in some cases, even death, precautions must be taken. But first, you have to know you have an allergy to take preventative measures against it.

To diagnose food allergy, a doctor must first make a differential diagnosis, that is, distinguish between food

A seafood meal can trigger an allergic reaction in sensitive individuals.

allergy and food intolerance or other conditions. He or she usually starts by taking a detailed patient history, then, like a detective, assesses timing of reactions, cause-and-effect relationships, patterns of eating compared to symptoms, and so on. Sometimes this process is sufficient to make a diagnosis.

In other cases, the doctor may ask the patient to keep a diary recording everything he or she eats and any subsequent reactions. If a pattern exists, it'll emerge. The next step is then the elimination diet: removing suspect foods one at a time to see what happens. If a food is eliminated and symptoms disappear, then it's likely an allergen. To double check results, the food may be reintroduced into the diet, under the doctor's direction, and when symptoms return, the diagnosis is confirmed.

Dairy products like cheese can trigger allergic reactions.

Surprised!

If the patient history, food diary, or elimination diet indicate specific food allergies, the next step is allergy testing. These tests measure any allergic response to suspected allergens. (See chapter 6, Tools and Treatments, for more on allergy testing.)

Only eight items account for 90 percent of all food-related allergic reactions in America:

- milk and milk products (milk, cheese, ice cream, etc.)
- eggs
- peanuts
- tree nuts (walnuts, cashews, almonds, etc.)
- shellfish (shrimp, crab, lobster, etc.)
- fish
- wheat and wheat products (cereals, breads, crackers, etc.)
- soy

Interestingly, the foods to which people react most often are foods common to their culture. In Japan, for example, rice allergies are more prevalent than they would be in Canada or the United States. In Scandinavia, codfish allergies are widespread.

Cross-reactivity is another concern with food allergies, particularly in certain food groups like tree nuts and shellfish. This condition is defined by sensitivity to all members of an entire food group, not just one specific food. For example, if someone has a history of allergy to shrimp, testing will usually show that the person is also allergic to crab, lobster, and crayfish: the entire shellfish food group. This is cross-reactivity. Consequently doctors often counsel patients to avoid similar foods to that to which they already have known allergic reactions.

Breathe Easy!

The most common reactions indicating food allergies are:

- itchy rash or hives
- swelling of the lips, tongue, face, and throat
- runny nose and sneezing
- headache
- dizziness
- shortness of breath
- wheezing
- abdominal pain
- diarrhea or vomiting

Although these reactions are mild for most people, for some the reaction can become very serious quite quickly. For these few people, even miniscule exposure to their food allergen can trigger anaphylaxis. Anaphylactic allergies cause a dangerous drop in blood pressure, which results in greatly decreased blood flow to the brain, heart, and lungs. Unconsciousness or even death can ultimately follow. Immediate medical intervention is mandatory. (Please see chapter 1.)

Completely Useless Fact

Under normal conditions, the human heart creates enough blood pressure to squirt blood up to thirty feet (approximately nine meters).

Most people with food allergies react to very few foods, usually less than four. Such isolated allergies make it possible to avoid problem foods while maintaining a reason-

> ## Celebrity Spotlight
>
> New York Ranger Tom Poti is allergic to peanuts and fish. His allergies didn't prevent him from medaling with the U.S. ice hockey team in the 2002 Winter Olympics, or keep him from turning pro and playing in the NHL.

ably normal diet. Take heart! Food allergies are one of the easiest to control.

First, learn to read food labels carefully and READ THEM. Educate yourself on the various forms and names of your allergen. For instance, if you're allergic to milk protein, you also need to search ingredient lists for sodium caseinate or casein, as both are milk derivatives. Or if you have a peanut allergy, you'll need to watch out for foods that contain **hydrolyzed** vegetable protein, which may contain peanuts. Don't accept foods from others (sharing from friends, for example) unless the food comes with a label which clearly lists ingredients. Avoid home-baked goods unless you can absolutely verify the contents. Avoiding food allergens is the best treatment for food allergies.

When dining out or eating at someone else's house, ask how food is prepared and about specific ingredients *before you taste anything*! And don't assume that because a food was safe the last time you ate there, it will always be safe. Ingredients sometimes change daily in food service establishments. Talk to your waiter, and if he doesn't have the answers to your questions, speak with the chef. Don't be shy. It's up to you to monitor the ingredients you might ingest. Your life could depend on it. (If you have severe food allergies, you should carry an epinephrine kit at all times. Please see chapters 1 and 6.)

ADDITIONAL FOOD ALLERGY CONCERNS

FOODS IN COSMETICS

Ingredients such as hydrolyzed soy, wheat proteins, hops, and other plant proteins are sometimes found in bath and skin-care products. Finely crushed nut shells are frequent additives in exfoliating creams. Many shampoos contain milk protein to encourage body, or egg proteins to add shine to the hair. Contact with these food ingredients could cause a reaction.

We readily absorb proteins through the skin, particularly when it's wet. While contact with food proteins in cosmetic products can result in the proteins being absorbed, any reaction would most likely be mild, causing only minor irritation such as hives. Still, there is a slight possibility that more severe reactions can occur. It's best to avoid all allergens completely, regardless of form. Read cosmetic labels carefully.

DATING AND FOOD ALLERGIES

Even if you don't eat or handle any food to which you're allergic, your date might. Please keep in mind that close contact with someone who has recently touched or ingested one of your allergens can trigger a mild reaction in you. Talk to your date about your allergy. Be open and honest; there's nothing to be ashamed about. Then make sure your date washes his or her hands thoroughly after eating and before any close contact.

Food Allergies: Fact or Fiction?

- *Food allergies are common.*
  FICTION! Although up to 25 percent of adults think they're allergic to certain foods, under three percent have diagnosable food allergies.
- *Milk allergies are common.*
  FICTION! Most adults who have trouble with milk or milk products have lactose intolerance, not a true milk allergy.
- *People with food allergies are allergic to many foods.*
  FICTION! Most people with food allergies are allergic to less than four foods.
- *Food allergy is either lifelong or outgrown.*
  FICTION! Young children usually outgrow allergies to milk, eggs, soybean products, and wheat often by age six or seven. However, allergic individuals rarely "outgrow" allergies to peanuts, tree nuts, fish, and shellfish.
- *Allergy to food dye is common.*
  FICTION! Bad reactions to food dyes are rare, fewer than one of every 500 adults.

What about kissing? Kissing can be risky business if your date eats shrimp and you're allergic to it. Kissing him or her right after eating could transfer shrimp proteins to your mouth and trigger a reaction. Make sure all traces of the allergen gets cleaned up before such intimacy. Flossing, brushing, and rinsing wouldn't hurt!

INJECTED ALLERGENS— BITES AND STINGS

There are two primary means of encountering injected allergens: needles and bites or stings. First let's examine bites and stings.

Mary was having a great time at the music festival, until she was stung by a bee. Knowing allergies ran in her family, but never having been stung, she made her way to the medical tent as quickly as she could. Mary didn't know how her body would react.

"This sting isn't the sting to worry about," the nurse casually informed her when he learned that she'd never been stung before. "The next sting is."

Injected allergens are no different from inhaled or ingested allergens in that you must have been exposed previously to the allergen before any adverse reaction can occur. The difference with bites and stings lies in that *everyone* reacts to the toxic effect of insect or other venom. Some people—an estimated two million Americans—also develop severe allergic reactions to such bites. That's the problem.

Very sensitive people may develop severe hives, swelling in the throat, difficulty breathing, nausea and vomiting, anaphylaxis, and even confusion or severe anxiety. Mildly sensitive people may only have hives and intense itching or pain around the site. Because the allergen is, in essence, injected, symptoms usually begin immediately or at least within a few minutes of the bite or sting.

What are the most common culprits? Bees, wasps, hornets, spiders, fire ants, and yellow jackets are the worst offenders. Certain species of snakes and scorpions run a close second. These stings or bites may cause some swelling and itching, but the site can remain painful for hours, even days.

Rapid reactions are usually more severe and require immediate intervention. (An EpiPen or an equivalent is sometimes required. Please see chapters 1 and 6.) Symptoms that take up to a few days to develop seem to be less severe.

Once you've been stung, the pain of mild insect or reptile bites can be treated with a baking soda paste. You can also apply a cold, wet cloth to the area to relieve any hot or burning sensation. OTC products like **hydrocortisone** cream or antihistamine sprays like Benadryl® can help reduce itching.

Bee stings can cause dangerous allergic reactions in some people.

Breathe Easy!

Many people are sensitive to stings or bites without even knowing it. The key is prevention once you do know. Avoid walking barefoot outdoors. Never disturb beehives or nests. Avoid sunny, rocky areas where snakes love to bake. Keep garbage cans and recycling bins tightly covered, particularly in late summer/early fall, to avoid attracting bees. (Also never leave soda cans or cups of other sweet drinks unattended outdoors. You might swallow a bee!) The point is to discourage unwanted encounters.

Injected Allergens—Shots, Vaccines, and IVs

The three steps in developing a drug allergy are the same as with all other allergens: (1) the person is exposed to the drug, (2) the person's immune system develops antibodies to the drug, and (3) the person is re-exposed to the same drug, and this time allergy symptoms occur. Some drugs that commonly cause allergic reactions are:

- penicillin-based antibiotics (like Amoxicillin®)
- sulfa-based antibiotics (like Bactrim®)
- certain kinds of insulin (those that contain beef or pork protein)
- vaccines (some contain eggs)

Penicillin is perhaps the most common allergy-producing drug. Reactions can indeed be serious and, as with most allergens, lead to anaphylactic shock. In fact, such reactions to penicillin cause more than 400 deaths

68

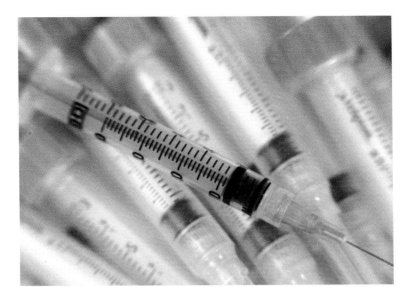

Some vaccinations and other injections may cause allergic reactions.

annually among Americans, making it a more common cause of death than food allergies.

More commonly, allergic individuals tend to react to drug allergies with skin irritations like hives. If you're one of them, make sure your doctor knows about the reaction as soon as it starts. He or she will likely take you off any medication immediately and change the course of treatment.

Sometimes hospital stays raise concerns. These fears are statistically unfounded. Only two percent of all hospitalizations result in allergic drug reactions. Yes, drugs are commonplace, but more often than not, any reaction isn't allergy related, and when it is, it's usually mild. In fact, truly *allergic* drug reactions account for only 5 to 10 percent of all adverse drug reactions in or out of the hospital, with skin reactions (like hives) being the most common form.

Breathe Easy!

Not many people actually develop drug allergies, but if you do, you should make sure any emergency information you carry indicates that allergy. It's critical for medical personnel to know about drug allergies before any treatment, emergency or otherwise. Carry a medical alert card or wear a Medical Alert bracelet indicating the allergy. If you can't inform the EMTs, the card or bracelet will.

Contact Allergies

Contact allergies are allergic reactions triggered by a person's skin coming into contact with an allergen. Simple, right? These reactions are usually caused by nickel, fabric softeners, detergents, rugs, deodorants, foam insulation, and plants like poison ivy, poison oak, and sumac. Contact with such allergens usually produces itchy rashes, hives, and weeping blisters.

Sometimes a rash can look more like eczema. Maybe you've noticed red, irritated patches forming on your elbows and behind your knees, and you remember that you recently changed laundry detergents. More commonly, raised, itchy bumps suddenly appear. For example, sitting on the floor at a friend's house, his dog is all over you, licking your chin and rubbing against your neck. The next thing you know your chin is itchy and has bumps all over it. In both scenarios, your skin simply touched the culprits, and contact allergies kicked in.

One of the more severe contact allergens is latex. Latex is a natural rubber that comes from a milky liquid found in rubber trees. This liquid is used to manufacture hundreds of rubber products we use at home and school.

70

Contact with a pet can sometimes trigger an allergic reaction.

Breathe Easy!

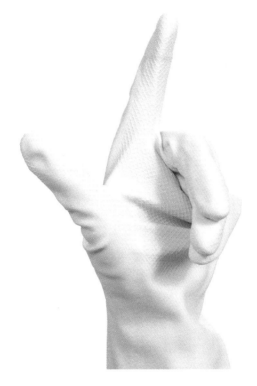

Some people are allergic to the latex in rubber gloves.

Rubber bands, condoms, balloons, sanitary pads, adhesive tape, bandages, tires, and rubber toys are just a few.

The medical and dental communities are heavy users of latex-containing products. Items such as disposable gloves, catheters, and material to fill root canals are common sites in medical offices. Depending on how they're actually manufactured, latex products can range from benign to hazardous in the allergic world. Gloves, balloons, and condoms are among the worst allergens in the latex family, but the capacity of these products to cause allergic reactions varies according to brand and production lot. Generally there are two types of allergic reactions to latex. The first is contact dermatitis, a poison ivy–like rash that develops within thirty-six hours after contact with latex. This condition is most common on the hands of individuals who regularly wear latex gloves, like those who do at work. It can, however, appear on other parts of the body following contact. An outbreak on an allergic man's penis after wearing a latex condom is not unusual. Although irritating, the reaction is not life threatening.

Immediate reactions, the second type, are potentially the most serious. Itching, redness, swelling, sneezing, and wheezing can occur. Rarely, anaphylactic shock sets in.

Severity of immediate reactions depends on the degree of sensitivity to latex and the level of exposure. The greatest danger occurs when latex touches thinner-skinned, moist areas of the body, like the lips, because more allergen is absorbed into the body more quickly. For someone with a latex allergy, blowing up balloons could be devastating!

It's estimated that at least one percent of the American population has latex allergies. However, certain groups of people are at higher risk. The most severe reactions seem to occur in health-care settings, where 10 to 15 percent of health-care workers have latex allergies. Even among nonmedical adults, the risk of developing sensitivity to latex may be as high as four or five percent of the population.

As you can see, ingested, injected, and contact allergies are many. The symptoms they trigger are just as diverse. One symptom we have yet to discuss—and one that is common to all allergens, but particularly inhaled ones—is asthma.

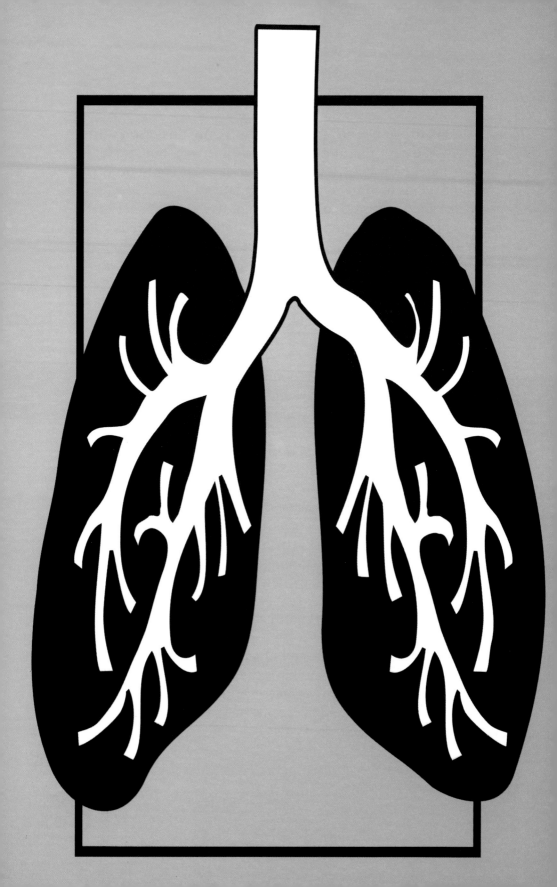

4

STRUGGLING FOR AIR:
The Biology of Asthma

Dee has a cold. She's had it forever. At least is seems that way. Now she's wondering if it's something more. She coughs all the time, but doesn't produce any **phlegm**, and her chest feels really tight. She can even hear faint whistling sounds when she exhales. What's going on?

Randy is throwing the Frisbee® with friends and doesn't seem to notice that he can't run as far or as long as usual without getting winded and coughing a lot. His friends do. They think he's out of shape.

For Brad, fall is always a killer. Walking on campus is miserable, but this year his allergies have been even worse. Brad isn't just itching, sniffing, and sneezing; this year he feels like he can't breathe.

Nan just finished swim practice at school. Walking out of the aquatic center, she's greeted by cold, dry winter air. Suddenly it feels like a vice has gripped her chest.

Meet Dee, Randy, Brad, and Nan. All four are typical young adults. All four are healthy, active teens. And all four have asthma.

What Is Asthma?

Asthma, in simplest terms, is a disease of the respiratory system. The individual with asthma will—sporadically and chronically—have trouble breathing. Such episodes are called asthma attacks. According to the American Academy of Allergy, Asthma, and Immunology, more than seventeen million people in the United States alone have asthma, and the numbers are rising.

Asthma is fast becoming a major public health concern across the continent, counting for more school absenteeism than any other chronic condition. According to the Surveillance for Asthma, each year over fourteen million school days are missed due to asthma-related issues. For adults, asthma is the fourth leading cause of absenteeism in the workplace, resulting in nine million lost workdays per year.

The Centers for Disease Control and Prevention (CDC) reports that the estimated cost of treating asthma—just for those under age eighteen—is $3.2 *billion* per year. When you include all groups of patients, the cost is more than twice that figure. Nearly 500,000 Americans are hospitalized annually because of asthma, and about 10 percent of those—nearly five thousand—die. And get this: asthma is the only chronic disease (besides AIDS and tuberculosis) with an *increasing* death rate.

A child with asthma may need to inhale concentrated oxygen to combat an attack.

Breathe Easy!

Wow. Talk about gloom and doom! Clearly asthma is a serious condition. The good news is that if we understand it and can diagnose it, we can treat and manage it. The first step is understanding the disease.

What happens during an asthma attack? Why does it get so hard to breathe? First, let's look at how the respiratory system works.

The respiratory system is the mechanism by which you breathe. It's made up of your nose and mouth, your **esophagus**, the trachea (or windpipe), bronchi (mid-sized air tubes connecting your windpipe to the lungs), bronchioles (the smallest air tubes that look like tree branches), the alveoli (air sacs at the end of the bronchioles), the lungs, and the **diaphragm**.

Air reaches the lungs by first entering our bodies through the mouth and nose. This air travels down through the trachea, which ultimately divides into two large tubes called the bronchi. Each bronchus branches out into hundreds of smaller tubes called the bronchioles that feed into tiny air sacs—which make up the lungs—through which oxygen is absorbed into the bloodstream and carbon dioxide transferred out.

When most people inhale and exhale, the muscles around the air tubes (airways) are loose and relaxed, and the lining of the airways is very thin. These two factors permit airways to remain wide open, allowing air to efficiently move in and out of the alveoli. Consequently, air moves freely throughout the entire respiratory system as we breathe.

During an asthma attack, rubber-band-like muscles around the airways spasm (or tighten and constrict) while the lining of the airways swells and thickens. The tightening of the muscles that encircle the airways is called bronchoconstriction. The swelling, reddening and

78

Airing the Facts

- The prevalence of asthma is increasing world-wide in industrialized countries.
- Asthma is increasing across all age, sex, and racial groups.
- In the United States, fourteen Americans die each day from asthma.
- In Canada, about 500 adults and 20 children die of asthma each year.
- More females die of asthma than males do, and slightly more blacks die of asthma than whites.
- In the United States, the death rate for asthma has more than doubled in the last twenty years.

narrowing of these airways is called airway inflammation.

Increased mucus production also kicks in along the airways, further clogging the tubes. All these factors combine to make the bronchi and bronchioles narrower, less flexible, and even clogged. As a result, air flow is hindered, and it becomes hard to move air in and out of the lungs.

Asthma involves both bronchi and bronchioles but not the alveoli. Think of a hose. What happens to the water flow if you step on the hose or squeeze it? It's impeded and reduced to a dribble. Not much water actually reaches the pool you're trying to fill, and the pool itself remains the same, just empty.

Now imagine your airways are hoses, and the air you need to live is water. The alveoli are pools. Keep in mind, though, that in the hose example, water flow was limited to one direction: out. Breathing involves air movement in two directions. Interestingly, during asthma attacks, it's actually harder to breathe out (expire) than to breathe in (inspire). Why?

When you inhale, airways naturally expand as your diaphragm lowers and ribs ease out. In most cases, this expansion is significant enough that air can pass through even somewhat obstructed passageways. As a result, most asthmatics don't encounter difficulty breathing in.

When we exhale, the diaphragm slides back up into position and the ribs relax. Our lungs—and all their airways—return to their more compressed "at rest" state, so any obstruction becomes markedly more troublesome. Slightly constricted airways become even more restricted, impeding air's release. When less air is released, more air gets trapped inside the lungs, leaving little room for fresh air to come in. That's when we feel like we can't inhale.

Believe it or not, the process we just described can be normal, up to a point. Everyone's airways constrict somewhat when they encounter irritating substances like smoke or dust. But in the person with asthma, the airways are hyperreactive or hyperresponsive. This means that the asthmatic's airways *over*react to things that would normally be minor irritants to a nonasthmatic individual. (Sound familiar?) Some doctors have even coined a term for this sensitivity: "twitchy airways."

Even though all people who suffer with asthma have some degree of restricted breathing, not everyone experiences it the same way. Many people just cough and cough and cough. Others feel they can't catch their breath. Some experience pressure or tightness in their

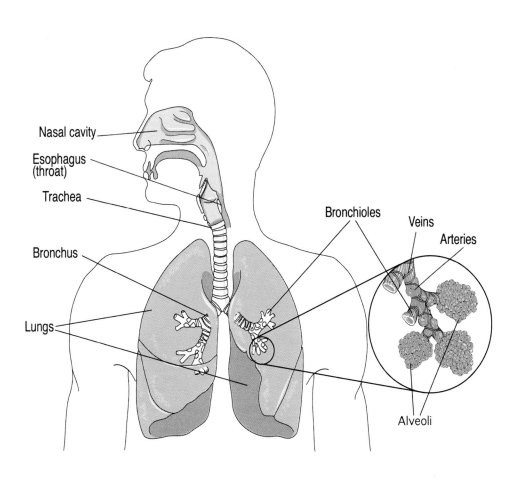

chest. Most wheeze to some degree, some more noisily than others.

Have you ever blown into the neck of a glass soda bottle? It makes a sound, doesn't it? Trying to squeeze air through narrow passageways produces a slight whistling or hum, much like when you try to force air out through pursed lips to whistle. In narrowed airways, that sound is commonly referred to as wheezing.

Because asthma symptoms can mimic symptoms of other illnesses, physicians sometimes treat them as if they were respiratory infections, not realizing the underlying cause is asthma. For the asthmatic, making a correct diagnosis is critical for two reasons: (1) you don't want to be medicated for an infection you don't have, and (2) asthma can be effectively treated—sometimes with virtually instant relief—if it's correctly identified.

Airway Inflammation

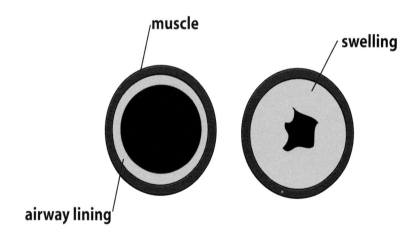

Normal   **Inflamed**

> ### More Completely Useless Facts
>
> • The average cough races out of the mouth at sixty miles (or ninety-six and a half kilometers) per hour.
> • The healthy human adult can commonly inhale between 200 and 300 cubic inches of air (an area 4 x 5 x 10 in. to 5 x 6 x 10 in.) in a single breath. That's between three and five liters! At rest, only about 5 percent of this volume is used.
> • During each twenty-four hour period, the average human breathes (inhales and exhales) about 24,000 times.

The process doctors use to diagnose asthma can involve most, if not all, of the following:

1. taking a detailed patient history including family history of asthma, known allergies, medical history, environmental living conditions, previous breathing difficulties and their context, school or work absences, emergency room visits, etc.
2. a thorough physical exam
3. chest X rays to eliminate other possible conditions
4. throat swab, blood tests, or **sputum** studies to rule out infection
5. a breathing test called spirometry or pulmonary function test (PFT) to measure the amount and rate at which air passes out of an individual's airways.

Breathe Easy!

Spirometry or PFTs are perhaps the best and most accurate diagnostic tools for detecting the presence of asthma (see chapter 6). Once a diagnosis is made, you're well on your way to recovery! That's the first step.

The second step is exposing your inducers, those things that trigger asthma attacks in you. Everyone is different. What causes an attack for one person may not trigger any symptoms in another. That said, some causes are more widespread than others, and most fall into one of three categories: exercise-, allergy- or infection-induced asthmas. We cover all three in the next chapter.

The better informed you are about your asthma triggers, and the more diligent you are in managing them, the less asthma will interfere with your everyday life. (Please see chapters 5 and 6 for management strategies.) Asthma doesn't have to control you! Many famous people—including athletes—not only survive asthma but thrive despite it. You can, too!

Even though there is currently no "cure" for asthma, it is not a progressively worsening or debilitating disease. Most individuals with asthma can maintain normal or nearly-normal lung function with appropriate treatment.

As common as it is, much remains to be learned about asthma, its causes, and how to prevent it. Researchers don't know for certain why some people get it and others don't. However, doctors have found that certain traits make it more likely a person will develop asthma. There are two primary ones:

- *Heredity*: To some degree, asthma seems to run in families. If your parents or any siblings have asthma, you are more likely to develop the condition than someone whose family does not.
- *Atopy*: A person is atopic when he or she is

Wonderful "Wheezers"

If you have asthma, you're in impressive company. Many accomplished athletes, musicians, actors, entertainers, writers, and even long-winded politicians have suffered with asthma and still achieved greatness. Here are a few:

Olympians (*medalists)
Bruce Davidson, equestrian
Tom Dolan, swimming*
Kurt Grote, swimming*
Nancy Hogshead, swimming*
Jackie Joyner-Kersee, track
    and field*
Bill Koch, cross-country
    skiing *
Greg Louganis, diving*
Debbie Meyer, swimming*
Jim Ryun, running*
Amy VanDyken, swimming

Leaders and Presidents
Calvin Coolidge
Che Guevara (Revolutionary
    leader)
John F. Kennedy
Walter Mondale
Peter the Great (Russian Czar)
Theodore Roosevelt
William T. Sherman (Civil
    War general)
Martin Van Buren
Woodrow Wilson

Musicians
Ludwig von Beethoven,
    classical
Judy Collins, folk
Alice Cooper, rock
Liza Minnelli, stage
Antonio Vivaldi, classical

Sports Stars
Jim "Catfish" Hunter, baseball
    Hall-of-Famer
Dennis Rodman, basketball
George Murray, Boston
    Marathon winner

Creative Types
Steve Allen, comedian
Loni Anderson, actress
Jason Alexander, actor
Charles Dickens, author
Bob Hope, comedian
Joseph Pulitzer, publisher
Martin Scorsese, director
Elizabeth Taylor, actress
Edith Wharton, author

Asthma medication is often administered through an inhaler like this.

prone to allergies. Remember, people often inherit a *tendency* toward allergies, not a specific allergy. That makes them atopic. For example, if your mom is allergic to shrimp, you won't necessarily be allergic to shrimp, too, but you may develop allergies toward other things like dust mites or pollen. If you think you are atopic, then you're at greater risk for developing asthma.

Despite the severity of health conditions it can cause, asthma is easily treatable and managed. Appropriate measures not only prevent and control asthma attacks, they can also allow a person to live a normal and active life. If you have asthma, it's critical to seek medical help. Schedule an appointment with your family doctor. He or she can guide you about what to do next. They may even refer you to an allergist or pulmonary (breathing and lung) specialist.

It is just as critical that you become aware of things in your environment that tend to make asthma worse. These elements vary from person to person, so it's important to become familiar with those factors that affect your particular condition. In the next chapter, we explore the most common.

5

STUMBLING BLOCKS:
Asthma's Triggers

Have you ever babysat a toddler? Maybe you have younger brothers or sisters. Little children are challenging, aren't they? The youngest among us can get into very serious danger very quickly, sometimes before we realize it.

Johnnie wanders into the street; Susie reaches up for a pot handle sticking out from the stove; Bobby loves taking a bath and turns on the water—just the hot. Kids require constant attention and definite "childproofing." What happens if we lapse in our attentiveness to them? The consequences can be injurious or fatal.

Asthma is somewhat like these kids. It, too, needs constant supervision and even a bit of "asthma-proofing." It can "get into trouble" before we know it, and if we lapse in our management of it, the consequences can be just as debilitating, even deadly.

How does one "asthma-proof?" As we said in the last chapter, the first step is correct diagnosis. The second step involves identifying triggers (or inducers), then taking steps against them. We previously learned that most asthma inducers fall into three broad categories: allergies, infection, and exercise. There is also a fourth area we have yet to discuss: occupational asthma. Let's examine each one.

Allergy-Induced Asthma

Since you already know how allergies work (from the first three chapters), suffice it to say that allergy-induced asthma functions much the same way. As IgE antibodies attack allergens, histamine and leukotrienes are released. These chemicals cause our allergic reactions.

It's important to note here that not everyone with allergies develops asthma, and not all asthmatics have allergies. But fully 80 percent of asthmatics do, so allergy-induced asthma is common. In such cases, besides sneezing, itching, and other symptoms common to allergic reactions, histamine and leukotrienes also trigger symptoms in the respiratory system. Hyperresponsive airways constrict and swell. Combine this response with allergy-induced inflammation and mucus production, and difficulty breathing quickly sets in.

The best approach to preventing allergy-induced asthma attacks, or any other allergy symptoms for that matter, is minimizing exposure to offending allergens. (Please see chapters 2 and 3.) Depending on the severity of symptoms, a maintenance program of oral or inhaled medications may also be necessary. (Please see chapter 6.)

Oral medications may be used to treat asthma.

Infection-Induced Asthma

Most people with asthma have acute episodes from time to time. How can you tell what causes them? One clue is the rapidity with which symptoms take hold. Episodes brought on by allergies tend to develop quickly; infection-induced attacks usually begin slowly, with other signs of infection, over a few days.

Viral or bacterial infections cause gradual deterioration in preexisting asthma as the infection gets stronger. Infections irritate the airways, nose, throat, lungs, and sinuses, aggravating already hyperresponsive airways. The added irritation often triggers asthmatic responses, but not right away. As with most symptoms of infection, the irritation takes time to build enough to trigger the response.

Respiratory viral infections (colds) are one of the most common causes of asthma. If you find yourself starting to feel under the weather, pay particular attention to respiratory symptoms. You may be primed for an attack. Flu shots are generally recommended.

Exercise-Induced Asthma

This type of reaction is commonly referred to as "EIB," or exercise-induced bronchospasm. No simple answer exists as to why exercise can create breathing difficulties for asthmatics and others. One main theory seems to stand out: when an individual exercises vigorously, he or she tends to breathe more quickly and deeply, in and out through the mouth. Such breathing causes (1) cooling in the airways, and (2) drying of the airways. These two factors likely cause EIB.

Cooling and drying of the airways stimulates mast cells (already in airway linings) to produce a chemical substance called a mediator, which causes the rubberband-like muscles encircling each airway to spasm. The muscles constrict, tightening around the airway much like our fingers would grip and squeeze a hose. That's a bronchospasm.

Perhaps the most important factor in this process is "mouth" breathing. When we breathe through our mouths, air passes directly into air passageways without having to go through the warming, humidifying, filtering effect of the nose. In fact, air that travels through the mouth, bypassing the nose, is moistened to only 60 to 70 percent relative humidity before reaching the lungs; nose-breathing warms and moistens air to about 80 to 90 percent humidity. No wonder the bronchi and bronchioles cool and dry as we exercise!

EIB is common for those with diagnosed asthma. Eighty to 90 percent of asthmatics have difficulty breathing with vigorous exercise. A lesser percentage exists for those who otherwise do not have asthma. Fifty percent of those with hay fever or allergic rhinitis (runny itchy nose, no asthma) and 10 percent of normal athletes have been found to develop EIB. For this reason, exercise-induced bronchospasm describes such episodes more accurately than exercised-induced asthma. Some EIB sufferers don't have asthma at all.

The signs of EIB are usually obvious: wheezing, shortness of breath, and chest tightness exclusively affiliated with vigorous exercise. This does not, however, refer to the windedness everyone feels when out of shape and trying to run the mile! It's easy to tell the difference. EIB has very distinct patterns. There are three stages: the

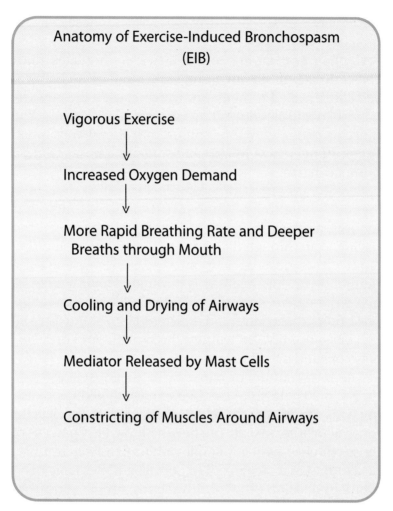

Anatomy of Exercise-Induced Bronchospasm
(EIB)

Vigorous Exercise

↓

Increased Oxygen Demand

↓

More Rapid Breathing Rate and Deeper
Breaths through Mouth

↓

Cooling and Drying of Airways

↓

Mediator Released by Mast Cells

↓

Constricting of Muscles Around Airways

early phase, the refractory (or grace) period, and the late phase. The early is the most severe.

The early phase of EIB can begin fifteen minutes into exercise, but most typically sets in after exercise ends. (Simple windedness occurs *during* the workout and eases up once you stop.) EIB generally peaks about ten minutes after exercising and lasts thirty to sixty minutes. It can eventually resolve on its own.

The severity of EIB is measured using the same tests employed in determining asthma's severity, that is, by measuring how quickly and forcibly air is expired with spirometry. (See chapter 6.) Genuine EIB is defined as a 15 percent (or more) decrease in such capacities within three to fifteen minutes (usually ten) following exertion. By comparison, most healthy subjects—those without EIB—commonly experience only a 10 percent (or less) drop in expiration capacity. A 20 percent decrease (or less) is considered a mild EIB episode. A 20 to 40 percent decrease in expiration-capacity is considered moderately severe, and a 40 percent or greater decrease is severe.

Remember, exercise-induced-bronchospasms peak around ten minutes after exercising. If you're gasping for air throughout an exercise session, you're probably just out of shape. Here's a typical pattern for an EIB attack:

After the initial bout of EIB—the early phase—there can be a thirty- to ninety-minute period during which little or no bronchospasm occurs, hence the name of the second stage: the refractory or "grace" phase. This "reprieve" occurs in 50 percent of individuals with EIB.

Some competitors actually take advantage of the break in symptoms to compete. These athletes find that if they "push through" the early phase of EIB, when symptoms peak, they can actually run through the bronchospasm and finish out a race during the refractory period virtually symptom free. It's not a great idea.

The late phase of EIB is less severe than the early phase, but still evokes symptoms in those who encounter it. Some never experience late phase at all, but if symptoms do return, they usually do so within twelve to sixteen hours after exercise, are substantially less severe, and resolve within twenty-four hours.

Breathe Easy!

Besides the obvious wheezing, chest tightening, and shortness of breath associated with EIB, there are a few subtle symptoms. They include:

- consistently coughing after sports or jogging
- susceptibility to cold air, coughing a great deal after being out in the cold.
- feeling out of shape and winded regardless of fitness level
- having breathing difficulty with "dry" sports, but not swimming

Anatomy of Exercise- Induced Bronchospasm (EIB)

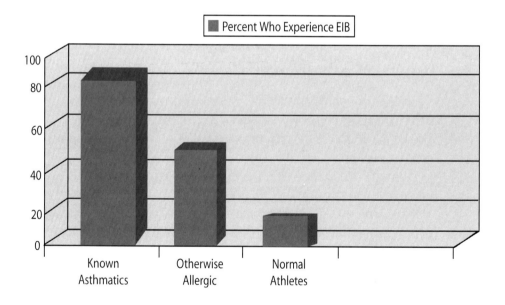

Because breathing cool, dry air is the key inducer of EIB, breathing warm, humidified air (for example, during indoor swimming) can completely or partially prevent EIB. Swimming is often the "sport of choice" for asthmatics and those with EIB. A warm, humid atmosphere, toning of upper body muscles, and the horizontal position of swimming—which helps prevent mucus from settling into the bottom of the lungs—are all positive factors to consider.

What other activities are well-suited to the EIB sufferer? Very light or nonaerobic activities like weight-training rarely result in EIB. Walking, casual biking, leisure hiking, and downhill skiing are also less likely to trigger an episode. Team sports that require short bursts of energy, such as baseball, wrestling, football, golfing, tennis, surfing, volleyball, gymnastics, and short-distance track and field events, are better choices for the EIB sufferer than sports requiring continuous exertion like basketball, soccer, lacrosse, field hockey, and long-distance running. Sustained, cold-weather activities such as cross-country skiing and ice hockey can also become problematic.

There's no such thing as the "perfect" exercise for the person with asthma or EIB. The key is selecting a sport you enjoy, whatever it is, and being smart about engaging in it. Here are a few tips:

- Work out in warm, humid environments.
- Breathe through your nose. If you must breathe through your mouth, try pursing your lips.
- Warm up! A good, ten-minute, warmup can lessen any chest tightness that occurs after exertion.
- Cool down! DO NOT STOP EXERCISE

97

ABRUPTLY. A warm-down period of ten minutes or longer, including stretching and walking, allows for gradual temperature changes in the airways.

- Restrict exercising if you have an infection, when temperatures are extremely low, or—if allergic—when pollen counts are high.
- Wearing a scarf or cold-air mask over the nose and mouth warms and humidifies the air before it reaches the airways. Make sure to do so in cold, brisk weather.

All of these things can help minimize EIB, but generally, inhaled medications taken prior to exercise are the most helpful in controlling and preventing exercise-induced bronchospasm. (Please see chapter 6 for specific medications and treatments.)

The Value of Exercise and EIB

You'd think that avoiding exercise altogether would benefit the person who struggles with EIB. Actually, the reverse is true. Regular exercise increases overall strength, endurance, and fitness and, if undertaken wisely, can result in less troublesome bronchospasms simply because the lungs are stronger.

For decades, it was thought that those with EIB or asthma shouldn't take part in any vigorous activities so as not to trigger an attack. What a shame! How many kids in the fifties, sixties, seventies, and even eighties sat on the sidelines because of EIB or asthma? Thousands did. We now know that such thinking is misguided.

Exercise not only improves physical health—and therefore EIB—it also impacts self-esteem, confidence, and psychological well-being. Today, with proper diagnosis and treatment, asthmatics and EIB sufferers can participate in and enjoy the benefits of exercise without fear. However, even today, a cycle of inactivity is far too common among people with breathing problems. Here's how it works:

1. Activity is restricted out of fear, ignorance or convenience.
2. Physical deconditioning occurs, and we become weaker and less fit.
3. Breathlessness from even mild effort increases because we're less fit.
4. Fear, worry, or concern sets in with normal breathlessness, so we further restrict our activity, and the cycle begins again.

This cycle repeats itself over and over until individuals give up entirely, thereby becoming completely inactive and genuinely unfit. In such cases, EIB is at its worst.

Having asthma or EIB does not mean you cannot exercise. According to a recent study, at least one in six athletes representing the United States in the 1996 Summer Olympics had a history of breathing issues. In fact, 117 out of 699 athletes reported having asthma or EIB. These conditions were most common among cyclists and mountain bikers. They were least common in volleyball, table tennis, and badminton. Interestingly, nearly 30 percent of the 1996 Olympians with breathing issues won team or individual medals in their sport, faring as well as those without breathing difficulties (29 percent).

Anatomy of Exercise- Induced Bronchospasm (EIB)

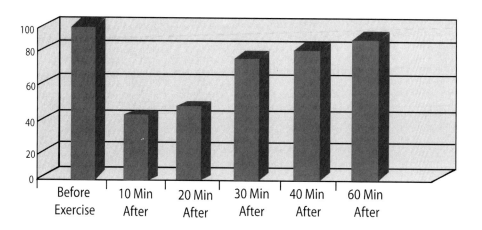

| ■ % Expiration Capacity | (90 to 100 is normal.) |

Even if you're not striving for Olympic gold, exercise is beneficial. All people with EIB or asthma should be able to exercise to their potential with appropriate diagnosis and treatment. That includes you.

Occupational Asthma

This is our final area of asthma triggers. It is also probably the least known and least discussed. Simply stated, occupational asthma is a lung disorder caused by inhaling particles, fumes, gases, or other potentially harmful substances while "on the job." Commonly, symptoms worsen through the work week, improve over days off, and recur when the employee returns to work. The pattern is often obvious.

Symptoms of asthma—wheezing, chest tightness, chronic cough, breathlessness—can appear for the first time in someone previously healthy, or childhood asthma thought to be long-gone may recur. Family history of allergies renders a person more likely to develop occupational asthma, but many individuals without such history still do.

The length of exposure that triggers this type of asthma varies with each worker and the specific contaminant. It can range from days to years. Once present, symptoms generally last for a long time, even beyond exposure to the irritant(s) that initially caused the reaction. Keep in mind that such reactions can be allergic or nonallergic. You don't have to be allergic to respond asthmatically.

Up to 15 percent of all asthma cases may have job-related factors. There are generally three categories of mechanisms that cause occupational asthma:

- *Direct irritants*: These irritants trigger symptoms immediately on exposure. They include strong substances like ammonia, sulfur dioxide, and hydrochloric acid. The reaction is definitely an irritant reaction, as opposed to an allergic reaction, since the immune system is not involved.
- *Pharmacologic mechanisms*: These irritants lead to a build-up of naturally occurring chemicals, like histamine or acetylcholine, within the lungs after prolonged, inhaled exposure. For example, chronic exposure to

Breathe Easy!

Common Culprits of Occupational Asthma

Job	Irritant/Substance
food processing worker	castor beans, papain, green coffee beans
baker, miller	cereal grains
veterinarian, animal handler	animal proteins
fisherman, seafood processor	animal proteins, seafood
health-care worker	latex, powdered proteins, medications
hospital worker	formaldehyde, glutaraldehyde
carpenter, forest worker	wood dust
lacquer or shellac handler	amines
hairdresser	persulfate
textile worker	dyes
janitor, cleaning staff	chloramine-T
solderer, refiner, jewelry maker	metals
electronic worker	fluxes
detergent worker, baker	enzymes
carpet maker, pharmaceutical job	gums
spray painter, insulation installer	isocyanates
adhesive handler	acrylate

certain insecticides used in agricultural work can result in an accumulation of acetyl-choline in the lungs, which, in turn, leads to asthma.

- *Allergens*: This type of occupational asthma usually sets in after long-term exposure to a work-related substance. Why? As with other allergies, the immune system needs time to build up antibodies to that particular allergen.

Identifying work-related triggers is critical. Once you've determined the source of your asthma, limiting exposure becomes a must. If you suspect occupational asthma, see your doctor. In some cases, medication effectively manages on-the-job irritants, but in others, complete avoidance becomes necessary. You might have to switch jobs within the establishment, or you might have to work somewhere else altogether.

According to the American Academy of Allergy, Asthma, and Immunology, occupational asthma has become the most prevalent work-related lung disease in the Western world, that is, in developed countries. Up to 15 percent of all asthma cases in the United States may be job related. Many workers, though, are misdiagnosed with chronic bronchitis. That can be tragic. If occupational asthma is not correctly diagnosed early, and the worker removed from exposure, permanent lung damage or changes can occur.

Obtaining a correct diagnosis is foundational to managing any condition. Let's look at how allergies and asthma can be diagnosed and managed. Read on.

6

SURVIVING ALLERGIES AND ASTHMA:
Tools and Treatments

We've covered allergies, common allergens, asthma, types of asthma, and asthma's triggers. Now that we understand what's going on, there has to be something we can do to feel better, right? Doctors can cure anything!

Well, actually not anything. There is no cure for either allergies or asthma, but there are things we can do to avoid both conditions, or at least alleviate and manage their symptoms. The first step is obtaining an accurate diagnosis. (We'll deal with allergies and asthma separately as we move along.)

Allergy Testing

If you suspect you're allergic to something—pollen, dust, mold, animals, foods, medications, etc.—see your doctor. He or she will likely send you to an allergist. Allergists are medical doctors who specialize in allergy and immunology, that is, they're trained in the prevention, diagnosis and treatment of problems involving the immune system. Since allergies are a direct result of an overzealous immune reaction, allergies fall under immunology.

What will an allergist do? Besides conducting a thorough patient history, he or she will probably recommend allergy testing to isolate your specific allergens. Don't worry; you won't have to study for these tests! Allergy tests are exactly what their name indicates: they're a tool for measuring exact substances that trigger allergic reactions in our bodies.

The most common allergy test is the skin test, or "scratch test," because it's rapid, simple, and for most people, quite safe. (In extremely allergic patients—those who have severe anaphylactic reactions—and patients with extensive eczema, skin testing cannot be done for obvious reasons.) Minute, diluted samples of each suspected allergen is placed just under the surface of the skin on the forearm or back, one allergen per site. Sounds painful, right? It's not. These samples are barely injected under the skin, so the process really doesn't hurt at all. However, specific sites can itch immensely within a few minutes if you turn out to be allergic.

If, within fifteen or twenty minutes, a red, swollen welt forms where an allergen was injected, the test is positive

---

Still More Completely Useless Facts

- The average surface of human skin is six-and-a-half square feet (or two meters square).
- Each square inch of skin contains approximately twenty feet (or six meters) of blood vessels.
- There are about forty-five miles of nerve endings on average in the skin of a human being. (No wonder we itch!)

---

for that allergen alone, indicating an isolated allergic reaction. You might develop only one welt out of eight or twelve pricks, or you might react positively to more. Everyone is different.

Unfortunately, taken by themselves, skin tests are not a completely reliable diagnostic tool. Usually doctors combine test results with the patient's description of when and how he or she manifests symptoms. For example, a doctor will diagnose a specific food allergy only when his or her patient has both a positive skin test and a history of reactions to that specific food.

For potentially allergic individuals in whom skin testing is not wise, doctors may recommend blood testing. The three most common blood tests for allergies are the RAST, CAP-RAST, and ELISA tests. These tests measure the presence of allergen-specific antibodies in the blood. If large amounts of a specific antibody are present, you're probably allergic to that allergen.

Blood testing is more accurate than skin testing, but it also has distinct disadvantages: results are not immediately available; tests generally cost more; and, in the case of food allergies, even with a positive result, the physician will likely order additional tests to confirm the results. For example, an elimination diet would likely be prescribed after a blood test to confirm potential food allergies.

An elimination diet requires removing suspect foods from the person's diet—"suspect" based on patient history, common food allergens, and positive results from previous allergy testing—until all allergic symptoms cease. Each food is then added back into the diet, one at a time, while a journal of reactions is kept. If symptoms recur following the addition of a specific food, that food is a likely allergen.

Another "confirming" test for food allergies is the double-blind food challenge. This test has become the crème-de-la-crème of allergy testing. Various foods—benign and potential allergens alike—are each placed in individual opaque capsules so the test subject doesn't know what he or she is ingesting. The patient swallows one capsule at a time while he or she is monitored for reactions during intervals after each ingestion. The advantage of this test is that if a patient has a reaction to only those capsules with suspect foods, and not to any other foods tested, the allergy is definitively confirmed. The disadvantages are that the tests are costly, and multiple food allergies are hard to evaluate using this procedure. Consequently, double-blind food challenges are not frequently done.

Whether skin, blood, or food elimination tests, allergy testing is the best way we know to diagnose and confirm allergies. All results, however, must be correlated to the individual's history of symptoms. Both are critical to a correct diagnosis.

Asthma and EIB Testing

You've done the allergy testing. You know you're allergic, but are you asthmatic, too? Doctors can test for all four types of asthma: allergy-, infection-, exercise- and occupation-induced.

To diagnose asthma, a physician typically does four things:

- obtains a thorough patient history, including any potential cause-effect pattern in breathing difficulties
- completes a thorough physical exam (including a chest x-ray, blood tests, and sputum studies to exclude other conditions)
- performs a baseline pulmonary function test (PFT) using either a peak flow meter or spirometer
- performs additional breathing tests following the introduction of potentially impacting factors (for example, perform a breathing test when the patient is at rest, at intervals during exertion, and then ten minutes after exertion

109

Breathe Easy!

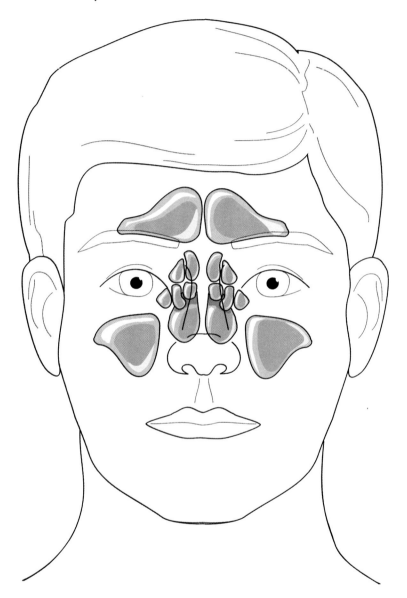

A person with asthma may also be prone to sinus infections.

if a doctor suspects EIB; or if chronic asthma is suspected, a patient is often tested before and after the introduction of a **bronchodilator** or other inhaled medication to measure the impact of such meds).

A spirometer is a machine that measures the volume and force with which air is exhaled (expired). Typically a patient is asked to take a deep breath and then blow as forcibly (and as long as they can using the same breath) as possible into a tube tethered to a small machine. The machine reads how hard the air was exhaled (force) and how much was expired (volume).

A peak flow meter works similarly, but only measures force (or flow), not volume. Comprised of just a short, plastic tube, the peak flow meter is a simple, portable, inexpensive device that effectively measures peak expiratory flow rate (PEFR). It is an indispensable tool in diagnosing and managing asthma.

A decrease of 15 percent or greater in PEFR is usually indicative of asthma regardless of the inducer (for example, EIB is defined as a 15 percent or more decrease in expiratory capacity following exercise; allergy-induced asthma is defined as a 15 percent or more drop in expiratory capacity after exposure to allergens; occupational asthma is defined as at least a 15 percent drop in PEFR after encountering irritants).

Healthy individuals without asthma consistently blow peak flows that vary less than 15 percent. Drastic swings in measurement shouldn't occur. Such comparative readings measure peak flow variability. The key is having an accurate baseline measurement with which to compare, then monitoring PEFR at various times.

MANAGING ALLERGIES
AND ASTHMA

Those are the asthma tests. Now you know if you have allergies or asthma and what triggers each of them. Where do you go from here? Management, including treatment, is the next step. Since we just discussed it, let's start with the peak flow meter as a management tool for asthma. Not only can peak flow meters diagnose asthma and EIB, they can also

- determine the severity of asthma
- monitor effectiveness of treatment during a specific attack
- monitor effectiveness of long-term treatment for chronic asthma
- detect changes in lung function indicating a needed adjustment in therapy.

Once you've established a personal best PEFR—when lungs are functioning at their healthiest or most normal—you want to maintain PEFR values within 80 percent of that number. That's the goal. To assist in monitoring these readings, allergists and immunologists have come up with a "traffic light" system to use as broad guidelines.

- Green Zone = 80 to 100 percent of normal PEFR: All systems go! (Maintaining current treatment, or even lessening it, is indicated.)
- Yellow Zone = 50 to 80 percent of normal PEFR: Caution! (Asthma is worsening, and a change in treatment is indicated.)

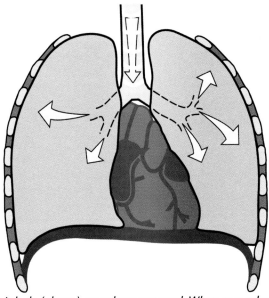

When you inhale (above), your lungs expand. When you exhale (below), they contract. A person with asthma may not be able to expel all the air in his lungs, which means he will have less room to inhale.

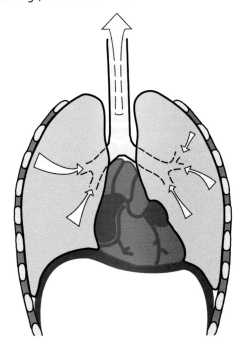

Fabulous Facts

- Immunotherapy is ultimately successful in up to 90 percent of patients with seasonal allergies.
- Venom immunotherapy prevents systemic reactions in insect-sting-sensitive patients 97 percent of the time.

• Red Zone = Below 50 percent of normal PEFR: Danger! STOP and take rescue medication immediately. Then call your doctor. (Your maintenance regimen will likely have to increase.)

A peak flow meter is to asthma what a thermometer is to body temperature. It simply helps you monitor what's going on inside your body. Like measuring a fever, taking your PEFR can determine when and how much medication is needed to first relieve symptoms, then to effectively manage them.

Allergy and Asthma Treatments

You've been diagnosed. You know your symptoms. How can you manage and treat your condition? There are commonly three techniques that doctors offer to help control allergies and asthma:

- avoid known allergens
- medication
- immunotherapy

Allergy and Asthma Medications

Condition/ Symptoms	Medication Type	Function
asthma—all types	anticholinergics (inhalant, oral, or injected)	Bronchodilator: prevents contraction (tightening) of underlying muscles of the bronchi.
asthma—all types	beta-2 agonists (for example, albuterol, pibuterol, terbutaline) (Inhaled)	Bronchodilator: relaxes muscle spasms in bronchial tubes.
asthma— allergy-induced	leukotriene receptor antagonists (oral tablets)	Bronchodilator: block leukotrienes, a chemical trigger of allergic response.
asthma— allergy-induced	anti-IgE (for example, Omalizumab) (injection)	Keeps IgE antibodies from attacking allergens by eliminating "free IgE" in the body.
asthma—all types	cromolyn sodium (nasal spray)	Anti-Inflammatory: prevents airways from swelling in response to allergens or cold.
chronic asthma	corticosteroids and glucocorticoids (for example, flovent) (inhalant)	Anti-Inflammatory: reduces swelling in bronchial tubes and enhances function of bronchodilators.

Allergy and Asthma Medications (cont.)

Condition/ Symptoms	Medication Type	Function
allergies	corticosteroid (nasal sprays, topical ointments, pills, injections and oral inhalers)	Anti-Inflammatory: reduces swelling and inflammation of nasal passages and airways, sinus cavities, and, if topical, localized areas of inflammation.
allergies	antihistamines (for example, Benadryl®) (oral, topical, injected, or nose spray)	Prevents the effects of histamine, thereby reducing allergic symptoms.
allergies	decongestants (oral, nose sprays, and nose drops)	Reduces nasal and sinus congestion by shrinking blood vessels, thereby decreasing the amount of fluid in mucus.
allergic anaphylaxis (particularly due to food and insect stings)	adrenaline epinephrine (for example, EpiPen®) (injected: often self-injected)	Counters sudden and severe drop in blood pressure (and resulting lack of oxygen to all systems) by stimulating rapid increase of blood pressure.
severe allergies	immunotherapy (multiple injections of known allergens over months or years)	Adjusts immune system to identified allergens—thereby desensitizing its reaction—through recurrent, long-term, minute exposure to those allergens.

Obviously with allergies and asthma, the best management tool is avoiding known allergens or irritants altogether. That includes allergy-proofing your environment and taking other condition-specific measures previously covered. But, for most allergy and asthma sufferers, such actions are combined with medications to affect the best result. Talk with your doctor. He or she will customize a regimen for you.

The last technique, immunotherapy, is not for everyone. It's expensive, time consuming, and not without risk. This therapy consists of a series of injections of the actual substance(s) to which you're allergic. Sounds threatening, but by gradually increasing doses of allergen over time, your immune system is gradually desensitized to it.

Since both allergies and asthma are chronic conditions, they require continuous management. Doctors agree that the best way to manage either is to have patients actively involved in their treatment. Partner with your doctor.

The better informed you are about your allergies or asthma, the better you can take control. With proper circumstantial and medical intervention, most allergy and asthma suffers can:

1. enjoy a normal lifestyle, participating in virtually any activity they wish,
2. live life close to symptom-free, night and day, and
3. minimize required medical intervention, including medicines.

Those are the goals. Please don't let these conditions control you; instead, take control of your conditions! Then you, too, can truly breathe easy.

Adams, Francis V. *The Asthma Sourcebook: Everything You Need to Know.* Los Angeles, Calif.: Lowell House, 1998.

American Academy of Pediatrics. *The American Academy of Pediatrics Guide to Your Child's Allergies and Asthma.* New York: Villard, 2000.

American Lung Association Asthma Advisory Group. *Family Guide to Asthma and Allergies.* Boston, Mass.: Little, Brown & Co., 1997.

Bergman, Thomas. *Determined to Win: Children Living with Allergies and Asthma.* Milwaukee, Wis.: G. Stevens, 1994.

Brostoff, Jonathan. *Food Allergies and Food Intolerance: The Complete Guide to Their Identification and Treatment.* Rochester, Vt.: Healing Arts Press, 2000.

Engel, June. *The Complete Allergy Book.* Buffalo, N.Y.: Firefly, 1998.

Fanta, Christopher H. *The Harvard Medical School Guide to Taking Control of Asthma: a Comprehensive Prevention and Treatment Plan for You and Your Family.* New York: Free Press, 2003.

Gershwin, Eric M. *Taking Charge of Your Child's Allergies: The Informed Parent's Comprehensive Guide.* Totowa, N.J.: Humana Press, 1998.

Joneja, Janice M. Vickerstaff. *Dealing with Food Allergies.* Boulder, Colo.: Bull Pub., 2003.

Lennard-Brown, Sarah. *Asthma.* Austin, Tex.: Raintree Steck-Vaughn, 2003.

LeVert, Suzanne. *Teens Face to Face with Chronic Illness.* New York: J. Messner, 1993.

May, Jeffrey C. *My House Is Killing Me! The Home Guide for Families with Allergies and Asthma.* Baltimore, Md.: Johns Hopkins University Press, 2001.

Mindell, Earl. *Earl Mindell's Allergy Bible: Includes Hundreds of Conventional and Alternative Strategies and Treatments for Every Kind of Allergy.* New York: Warner Books, 2003.

Plaut, Dr. Thomas F. *Dr. Thomas Plaut's Asthma Guide for People of All Ages.* Amherst, Mass.: Pedipress, 1999.

Rowlands, Barbara. *Asthma and Allergies.* Pleasantville, N.J.: Reader's Digest, 1999.

Shepherd, Gillian. *What's in the Air? The Complete Guide to Seasonal and Year-round Airborne Allergies.* New York: Pocket Books, 2002.

Walsh, William E. *Food Allergies: The Complete Guide to Understanding and Relieving Your Food Allergies.* New York: J. Wiley, 2000.

Young, Stuart H. *Allergies: The Complete Guide to Diagnosis, Treatment, and Daily Management.* New York: Plume, 1999.

Zellerbach, Merla. *The Allergy Sourcebook: Everything You Need to Know.* Los Angeles, Calif.: Lowell House, 2000.

Allergy Be Gone (a private company for allergy
  information and products.)
www.allergybegone.com

American Academy of Allergy, Asthma and
  Immunology
www.aaaai.org

American Medical Association
www.ama-assn.org/ama/pub/category/1981.html
  (Adolescent Health Page)

Asthma and Allergy Foundation of America
www.aafa.org

Canadian Lung Association
www.lung.ca
www.lung.ca/asthma
www.lung.ca/asthma/allergies

Food Allergy and Anaphylaxis Network
www.fankids.org (Food Allergy News for Kids Page)
www.fankids.org/FANTeen (Food Allergy News for
  Teens Page)

How Stuff Works
www.howstuffworks.com
www.howstuffworks.com/allergy (Allergy Page)
www.howstuffworks.com/immune-system (Immune
  System Page)

National Institutes of Health—National Library of
  Medicine
www.nlm.nih.gov/medlineplus (Health Information
  Page)

Palo Alto Medical Foundation
www.pamf.org

University of Iowa Health Care
www.uihealthcare.com/topics (Health Library Topics A–Z)

Publisher's note:
The Web sites listed on these pages were active at the
time of publication. The publisher is not responsible for
Web sites that have changed their addresses or discon-
tinued operation since the date of publication. The publisher will review and update the Web sites upon each
reprint.

adrenaline kit An emergency kit containing adrenaline and other allergy medication to be used in case of a sudden, unexpected exposure to an allergen that causes life-threatening symptoms.

allergists Physicians trained in the prevention, diagnosis, and treatment of problems involving the immune system.

alleviated Eased, lessened.

antibodies Protein molecules that circulate throughout the body neutralizing and eliminating harmful substances.

arachnids (uh-RAK-nids) A group of invertebrates that includes spiders, ticks, and scorpions.

atopic (a-TOH-pik) A tendency for excess inflammation in the skin and the linings of the nose and lungs. It often runs in families with a history of hay fever and other allergies.

benign Harmless.

bronchodilator Drug that releases bronchial smooth muscle to ease breathing.

cardiac arrhythmia An irregular heartbeat, sometimes a symptom of an allergic reaction to something.

chronic (KRON-ik) Long lasting or frequently recurring.

dander Minute scales of hair, feathers, or skin.

dehumidifier A device that helps to remove excess moisture from the air.

diaphragm (DI-uh-fram) A muscle partition that separates the chest and the abdominal cavity.

diverse Varied; having different characteristics.

dyspnea (DISP-nee-uh) Shortness of breath.

eczema (EK-zuh-muh) A skin condition characterized by redness, itching, and oozing from lesions.

electrostatic filter A mechanism that uses electrically charged particles to remove potentially harmful particles from the air.

EpiPen® An autoinjector that provides the person having a life-threatening allergy reaction an emergency dose of epinephrine (adrenaline).

esophagus (ee-SOF-uh-gus) The tube through which food passes on its way to the stomach and other parts of the digestive system.

fungi Parasitic, spore-producing organisms that include mold, mushrooms, yeast, and rust.

HEPA air filter A high-efficiency particulate absorption filter that purifies and removes potentially harmful particles from the air.

hives Raised patches of skin that cause intense itching; usually caused by exposure to an allergen.

hydrocortisone (hi-droh-COR-ti-sone) A medication, similar in construction to adrenaline, that can help reduce swelling and irritation; often in the form of a skin ointment when used to treat allergic reactions.

hydrolyzed (HI-droh-lized) Something that has had hydrogen added to it.

immune system The body's system that protects against foreign substances, such as bacteria or allergen, by producing antibodies.

inflammatory A localized protective reaction of tissue to irritation, infection, or injury characterized by redness, swelling, and pain.

lactose A sugar present in milk.

lesions (LEE-zhuns) An abnormal change in a body's structure or organ due to injury or disease.

mediators The agent that helps bring about a physical, chemical, or biological response.

mildew A surface discoloration caused by fungi.

miticides (MITE-i-sides) Products used to kill

mites.

organic Relating to living things.

phlegm (flem) Mucous secreted in abnormal quantity in the respiratory system.

potent Strong, powerful.

proliferate Increase; grow.

propagation Increase, spread.

propensity A sometimes intense natural tendency to do or have something.

ragweed Any of a variety of North American weedy herbs that produce pollen and are highly allergenic.

relative humidity The ratio of the amount of water vapor actually in the air to the largest amount possible at the same temperature.

rhinitis (RINE-ite-is) Inflammation of the mucous membrane inside the nose.

seizures (SEE-zhurs) Sudden attacks of convulsions; sometimes results in a loss of consciousness.

sensitized To have a higher than average reaction to something.

shock A sudden physical reaction characterized by a rapid drop in blood pressure and other vital processes.

spore count The amount of pollen and mold spores in the air as measured by air sampling equipment.

sputum A mixture of saliva and discharges from the respiratory system that is coughed up.

tannic acid A white or yellowish powder derived from the bark or fruit of many plants and trees.

teem To become filled; overflowing.

PICTURE CREDITS

Artville pp. 10, 32, 54, 88, 104
Autumn Libal p. 43
LifeART pp. 74, 81, 110, 113, 113
Photos.com pp. 13, 16, 23, 35, 47, 48, 59, 60, 67, 69,
 71, 72, 77, 86, 91
Benjamin Stewart p. 82

The individuals in these phtographs are models, and
 the images are for illustrative purposes only.

Jean Ford is a freelance author, writer, award-winning illustrator, and public speaker. She resides in Perkasie, Pennsylvania, with her husband of twenty years, Michael, and their two adolescent children, Kristin and Kyle. Internationally recognized, her work includes writing for periodicals from the United States to China, and speaking to audiences from as close as her tri-state area to as far away as Africa. Although she generally writes and speaks on nonfiction topics, Jean also enjoys writing and illustrating children's books.

Dr. Carolyn Bridgemohan is an instructor in pediatrics at Harvard Medical School and is a Board-Certified Developmental-Behavioral Pediatrician on staff in the Developmental Medicine Center at Children's Hospital, Boston. She specializes in assessment and treatment of autism and developmental disorders in young children. Her clinical practice includes children and youth with autism, hearing impairment, developmental language disorders, global delays, mental retardation, and attention and learning disorders. Dr. Bridgemohan is coeditor of "Bright Futures: Case Studies for Primary Care Clinicians: Child Development and Behavior," a curriculum used nationwide in pediatric residency training programs.

Dr. Sara Forman graduated from Barnard College and Harvard Medical School. She completed her residency in Pediatrics at Children's Hospital of Philadelphia and a fellowship in Adolescent Medicine at Children's Hospital Boston (CHB). She currently is an attending in Adolescent Medicine at CHB, where she has served as Director of the Adolescent Outpatient Eating Disorders Program for the past nine years. She has also consulted for the National Eating Disorder Screening Project on their high school initiative and has presented at many conferences about teens and eating disorders. In addition to her clinical and administrative roles in the Eating Disorders Program, Dr. Forman teaches medical students and residents and coordinates the Adolescent Medicine rotation at CHB. Dr. Forman sees primary care adolescent patients in the Adolescent Clinic at CHB, at Bentley College, and at the Germaine Lawrence School, a residential school for emotionally disturbed teenage girls.